city of destiny

David Lloyd Whited

poems by David Lloyd Whited

arranged for publication by dan raphael

isbn 1-878888-75-7

nine muses books   nine muses mystery theatre
3541 kent creek road, winston oregon 97496
ninemusesbooks999@gmail.com
ninemusesbooks.vispo.com

designed by margareta waterman and dan raphael

This book is dedicated to Daniel & Ingrid, brothers, sisters & parents, poet friends & social service friends. Thank you for the love, inspiration & friendship you shared with David throughout his life.

I am especially grateful to dan raphael and margareta waterman for publishing *City of Destiny*.

Marian Whited

publisher's note

when a poet dies, the poems show clearer, stronger, more beautiful. the poet's living presence no longer distracts, the poet's immortal presence rings and sings in the poems.

David left us before we were even thinking of his not being around. "too young, too young" in my heart, being myself some years older and still alive. "the real one is still to come" he whispered to me through the phone, as we finished up with *Olde Man Coyote Goes to Towne, "City of Destiny,* that's the one."

and then we lost him. now we have *City of Destiny.* for him, my heart knows, a fair deal. poetry is for the world. we have had a living David Lloyd Whited, now no longer. we now have his poet's voice, clearer stronger more beautiful.

the real things he saw, the gentle tender voice, the total compassionate non-judgement that sees what might be judged, but refrains, doesn't care, lets it all be. and the pen holds it all, metes it out line after line telling what he knows -- showing what shows itself to him. his mind, his emotions, the world's ways, the feelings and travails of others and self. in a setting of living earth, filled with creatures to talk with and learn from and be struck with their beauty.

> *. . . as pretty as a quail*
> *and few things are*

margareta waterman

margareta waterman

City of Destiny

Table of Contents

I: On the Avenue

Most of the time he is packed	23
Down on The Avenue	24
The Killdeer	25
Finding those Republican Guards	26
Real Estate Training	27
Economic Recovery	28
"Seventy percent of the dust in a house is human skin"	29
Overlooking the flooded fields, the reported	30
A rose for the sea	31
Health Department lady knows what she knows…	32
My resume recounts all the things I once was	34
"those who must be watched are assigned to each other"	35
A sawed off dudeen	36
transcendensity!	37
there we wuz noshing hors d'oeuvres when . . .	38
generally helpless on the page	39
the sun drifts toward raw meat, raw heat of	40
loved beyond the fade, jaded may not be	41
Kimboed	42
FOUR VIEWS OF THE DESERT	43

from Charles Baudelaire
    Our Ennui
    Her Ennui
    His Ennui
    Their Ennui

II: Island of Destiny

unbuilding the bone, remembering   51
Following the Equinox   52
"I do not write to kill time"   53
"every poem is time, and burns. ."   54
"you were born to live on an island"   55
"Poetry, suspension bridge between history and truth"   56
Ground glass to dogs while the painted smiles   57
presiding over a government of birds. unbreakable   58
crossing the street, standing on corners for no   59
wavering between doubt & faith drinking the rain   60
the fish's fin cutting the wake of water in the   61
The frogs reach out to us in the afternoon calling   62
neither love nor longing   63
Practicing the Yoga of Pain   64
Rimbaud left Uncollected   65

suffering and pleasure; black moons, white moons.
a shivering song which chants its measure
the wallpaper mildewed, the room filled with distractions
beneath a coraled archipelago of stars
the early morning avenue is cold & vacant
this astonishing chicken, astonished chicken announcing
"I called up executioners in order to bite
ankle deep in grass the star show falls

III: Trees are Tangled

Tangled up in Blue   77

There is some obscure boiling anger in the privacy   78

Choose again;   79

working in the garlic fields of hell   80

Sometimes you're the enduring wave of my   81

refracted by her light, by her cold motion to leave   82

each year may be a dungeon (with no key)   83

"Fragile Fox II to Fragile Fox I: 84

"The weaker the wine."   85

the woods dissolving into darkness at the top of the hill   86

revenge like a weight in the heart of steel   87

The crow raves   88

A Kind of Clear Negative   90

Sprinkling blossoms on the floor   92

The Unemployment Line on Venus   94

Left carrying ice to an argument   96

formaldehyde of hope to save it for tomorrow   97

The deadly birds of the soul are caught in the lights   98

Though trees are tangled in the light innocently   99

IV: Stars Tumble Out

"ruing alien firmaments"   103
"All are bound into a uniform edition, one can't be redeemed" 104
"twist & trout on salmon chanted evening"   106
having gone finally south   107
In the crosshairs   108
Hanging out down to Dead Puppy Beach   109
where wonder goes   110
"Harry the herd 'til a weak one drops"   111
Wiring the earth to the sky, & humans to town by cable tv.   112
In the shadows where the trilliums curl their petals   113
"I was sick as a trout"   114
this is not a pain free life: neither were we promised   115
"The words in a line of poetry are small. . ."   116
"dancing in the rags of an old remorse."   117
"The bones are lovely, dark and deep. . ."   118
"Life is cruel; that's the whole point."   120
"struck in the head with a sunflower."   121
"A few good things are left on earth."   122
a crack opens in the sky. stars tumble out   123
Life at the Muskrat Hotel   124
"The color of truth is grey."   126

V: Lost Boys

The universe is a vast system of poorly signed freeways.   131

Summer leads the rivers down from the mountains   132

A butterfly aching settles the end of summer   134

shadows twilit the walls of deckled brick grey   136

"when girls pout, make yourself available."   137

we all lay down. we all lay down & wait. we all lay down   138

she filled me like wet sand whispered   139

the famous temple   140

"Through this ugly duckling world."   141

Honest she took my shape & would not leave, could not   142

still searching for the lost boys   143

VI: This Brown Paper Bag

"We walk till we get to another time. and then we steal a vehicle" 159

night crawled up the front steps, a pure white cat 160

gone dizzy with hunger of love, & the mind gone 161

"these mad dogs of glory" & their lost toys 162

"I think I still have a bottle of poet left." 163

the social services 164

searching for "so called genius darlings who are not." 165

"The sun like a yellow glove" 166

I wake with glass silvered in my hair 167

breath like a mist of folded wing 168

a field, a fence, & darkness 169

"Each star a wave of flight" 170

These pastel women—even when the pen won't write. 172

"Except pornography is the cure for war . . ." 173

Gondwana mama! 174

unattainable (elegiac melancholy) 175

"Feed me to my prime: 176

The river shimmers & our eyes light. 178

"Throwing the china" 180

How it is that this brown paper bag is a ceremony? 181

VII: As they Always Have

"Woman is her own landscape . . ."   185
"naked, lonely & cold."   186
The herons are leashed to their shadows   188
the rain takes off its clothes, glues ours   189
stone upon stone wounding the alphabet   190
she spreads guilt in the night, built on   191
having learned to lie, we will   192
the stars are seeds in a garden of sky   193
I borrow the money to bury my father   194
things will turn up they always have   195
nates. Natez. Buttocks.   196
"abandon all hope when you enter me."   197
neap tide & a sea-raged landscape.   198
time fate, and strange ways   199
"a man, a woman, & a relationship.   200
" . . . what the gods mean by words   201
like scraps of sound balanced in the wind   202
reinventing & transforming   203
transparencies   204
Get It?   205
"lifting the spine   206
Carving the gods into wood, this way they will burn   207
Tracking Indian Creek   208

Editing my Brother's *City of Destiny*

If David were still alive it would be easier to separate him from his poetry. An elegant Beat, a civilized native, "I'm a creature of delicate sensibilities," he would say. But while the focus of this book is the poetry, the words are inextricable from the being who wrote them.

Going through the poems I wanted to add "Island" to the title, as more of the poems involve his life on Vashon, his domestic life and the natural world around him. The contrasts between the two, and the consistency of the author's tensions with both environments. The difference is with the urban environment the tensions are mostly external, while on the island he's working more with personal relations and deeper inner conflicts and perspectives. David looks like a city but has a wild-in-places island inside.

He spent boyhood in Umpqua OR (northwest of Sutherlin, north of Roseburg), near the river of the same name. "Umpqua means 'this is the place' or 'I'm tired let's stop here,'" David would explain. Having a place is essential to him, emphasized by his acquisitive nature (around 10,000 vinyl LPs), and he found that nest in 2.5 acres near the mouth of Judd Creek on Vashon. A chunk of these poems were written while renting a large, moldering house half a mile away. Others of the poems are set in an inland, northwest rural that could be Umpqua or other spots.

And the city. David was never a city boy which didn't mean he was naïve or harmless. For decades he worked in Tacoma, writing grants and running programs for the Puyallup Nation; this entailed his involvement with other health and welfare programs in the area. Most of his work was in the sad, mistreated, misunderstood parts of town and those who lived there.

David wrote copiously for a good while—in notebooks, matchbook covers, whatever paper handy. He didn't publish much, so much of what he wrote is unpublished, manuscripts like *The Mathematician* and *Pompeii*. *City of Destiny* was assembled in 1999.

Looked through this manuscript recently with margareta, getting some questions to answer, some format to clarify. Just reading a few lines here and there the emotional intensity of David's work and the precise twists in ordinary were & are so powerful. It can seem too easy, framed in an odd dialect, darlin', homey but seldom without a hint of irony or bitterness. David means everything he says, exactly.

Calling David's poems "accessible" is not to diminish them, their precision and bravery. An unlocked door could be as much a warning as a sign of generosity—everyday heartbreak & despair, everyday questions that always go unanswered.

A wink and a leer, a growl and a tear. He is the killdeer, not drawing attention from his young but from his own pains and needs, brown corduroy feathers concealing his inner ferocity and sorrow. Nothing indulgent or weepy here though, with David's precise control of language and tone. Like all fine art, the questions and contradictions of our lives are unresolvable. We do what we can—stay warm, drink, write, thrash out into the rainy night.

dan raphael

On the Avenue

Most of the time he is packed

He was camouflage clothing & flags.
She was wearing black, & the moon
was not a ghostly galleon. The tide
was washing high around the island.
He was into weapons: carried them
Kept them clean, oiled them well.
Kept his back straight, his German
hat tilted low. She drank white wine,
enough. He sipped his beer and dreamt
about her machine. the way she pursed
her lips. He took her home & showed her
his gun. chrome plated, glistening
cylinder – one chamber empty. He asked
her if she knew what to do with it.
If she could handle a gun. She took it
tumbled from his hands & his eyes glinted.
And she cocked he hammer back, gave him
this look of callous understanding;
placed the sleek chrome barrel in her
mouth. tired like and weary full.
His eyes lit frightened light
& he took the weapon back. careful.
one bright with killing & one with
total disregard for death. "that's
what it's for, isn't it?" she asked.
they live together now. & he
never asked her about pistols again.

Down on The Avenue

the tangled failure of the downtown
pacific avenue translucent hoboes
& the stranded mad drunk ill confused
by the constant emotional misfire
in their skulls, the inching slowness
of each perplexing idea.
how things don't change.

the medicated, the unmedicated, the self-medicated
totality of street people.
a stubborn clinging to life
with failing reason and dubious future.
alien to here and no fortunate place to go.
weaned on mushrooms and white port.
white bread at the white mission.
white light slowly draining out through the skin.
missionaries and their three-piece suits
and the shield of "The Watchtower" across their hearts
doing the pious distasteful duty
for the less fortunate. a lame assurance
that the afterlife will be better.

an idea. a seamless stone of desert:
the brainpan thoughts inching towards thinking
not even a migraine to be found.
the wind gives way, learning by injection.

there is no discarded surplus in heaven.
three squares and a warm place to sleep
right on top of those warm air grates of hell.
all those hot gospel songs to sing
in praise of the goodness of god
& the ultimate dispassion of the streets of gold.

The Killdeer

the killdeer frantic broken wing crying from the ground
the motionless sun cloaked in a shadowless sky
in which nothing moves but the bird's crimson fear.
the rugged dance of her wings filtering the truth
of the killdeer cry. like snow in April; like
a water spout funnel cloud on the mid-Sound;
like a full blown tornado. baseball size hail
here in this early northwest spring. the slap
crash violence of lightning. the thunder. all of it
filtering the truth of this bird's cry, the wing
which is not broken. wavering awareness of my own frail
shadow passing finally out of this dream. too small
too quickly. savor each day. and leave it well.
take only the knives & your fishing gear; all else
is illusion. & nothing else is yours. you can't even
trust your breath or your blood. & yeah.
the killdeer's lying about her wing.

Finding those Republican Guards

The Persian Gulf
Operation Desert Shield.
we own the night but
the mission is so top secret
that we don't know where we are.
we wander lost several hours
in this night we own
in this desert we don't
without even a compass.

we crest one more rise & dig in.
wait in miles and miles of darkness.
we pick them up on our infrared.
a large group assembling to our left
at the mouth of a ravine. They begin
advancing on our position. all hell
breaks loose. nothing but rockets and
rounds. explosions. they melt back
in retreat, a determined, well-trained
enemy. attacking and regrouping
all night. about oh-six-hundred we can
see the field of fire. By god,
nothing but dead and shattered
camels everywhere. trying to get to water.

buzz like a bee in a jar, hornet in a jar,
wasp in a jar, yellowjacket in a jar;
buzz like a bee in a jar; mud dauber in a jar,
bumblebee in a jar; buzz like a bee in a jar.
The war cry of yellow ribbons tied in bows.

Real Estate Training

the heart takes its own meaning, bends &
malleates the situations to fit what it understands
& expects. more sheep than eagles every time
confronted by the perplexities of this world, this life.

a shivering flame in the afternoon—dusk & fog plotting
their blending into night. which has the heart
of a raptor. This sliding away of winter, the slow
shrinkage of the Island. the landslides dabbling
their toes in Judd Creek. lamenting the loss of the
fine green sustaining root-binding foliage

the mood of the Island still—like gulls crying
the crows selling trinkets & bragging
stepping outside of the rhythm, out of the music

back in the city's
drab room at the top of the stairs in a sullen
apartment building. dark windows at the
drab end of a hopeless street, an empty man
sweats in his storming sleep. a star winks out
and its death arrives a thousand years too late
blossoms knowing the need & the ruin of rain
shape the word and break it into the air

& the crows, huh! they own everything
clicking their total disapproval
of not only your solvency, but your existence.

Economic Recovery

In a solitary sawmill town shrouded in fog
and living on unemployment, his wife quietly
went insane, wavering at the edge of poverty
stretching hunger to make the payments as
their dream of life folded itself back into
the water-soaked hills.

the wind hunts and snuffles
among the trees. sifting through dead leaves &
the moldy litter for traces of the desire it lost.
somehow, the tourist ants of summer will be tilting
their weight on the island, outboard skis breaking
the morning into small change and cold beers.
drinking the dazzle of life and overfilling the
County dump/landfill/solid waste disposal site

Shivering in the dazzle of increasing taxes, less
wild land, the deer attempt to cross the traffic
of Quartermaster Drive.

"Seventy percent of the dust in a house is human skin."

each decade wears itself thin, grows lean, empty,
and rolls on. Mallards dabbling with the gulls at
the mouth of the creek. glacial till still moving
towards the sea. The island keeps its wet secrets also.
the island aquifer a topic of debate & real estate
expansion. large profits. always an inexorable
dragging of the island into the sea.
May the old die in peace.

A flight of geese lost in the fog navigating
a wing and a honking while the water slaps
geese lost in the fog navigating
wing and a honking while the water slaps
fresh down to the sea. taking finally the long
slow way home. skirting the beach along this low sky
that breaks its knees crawling across the island.

Our lives spread out beyond us, beyond our control. rings
within the rings; expanding rings eroding the beach which
sets its tidal limits. Lurching through life with
the lilt of wine. blue & bitter as forgiveness
she turns her heels, averts her dark eyes
removes her hand & wears away.
the grooves, the patterns, the chips & cracks in
our lives are settling on the mantle;
though they make a pattern still.

Overlooking the flooded fields, the reported
disproportion, a city's desolation does not sleep.
Crossed by the moon & the city planning office
though endorsed by the mayor. government works
through and itch and squirm day. scant breakfast
quavering at the lip of the grave. still dancing.

morning kittens, half-grown tigers, chattering
to the loggy slow early spring fly at the morning bath.

the forest is a lost myth. the forester a jailer.
the logger disappearing, tracking the far trees.
snags of firs, like soldiers bent lower by the guns.
tools, heroes, and marines. the owls taking the fall.
the salmon mourning their losses, like fishermen.

out at the end of wind knuckle loop drive
lost continents are harbored in her eyes.
the scant ceremonials are still secret sins. frog noise
early afternoon at the swale.   the island, like the
jungle eats its dead. spring buds swell to blossom
the multiple uses of bitterness. the morning muse
of coffee.   Half-light & bird songs. late last
night she held the light as I buried that road-kill tiger.
this morning there is coffee, and it rains.

A rose for the sea

should we touch, the tribes of clouds would drag the
sky down for our comfort. It does not happen
quickly. it does not happen silently,
but do not blink.

ashes, dust, & dirt in love, profoundly in this desire
& lost in the desire to forget death, gravity, & time.
does my memory yet burn in your body?

the streets are an enormous web of desert
my mind is black and blue with solutions
guided by faithful amnesia, desire evoked
by death in a room too small to hold this dream.

desire dampens our lives, moistens the folds between us
this passion which will not, cannot take flame
though we are hungry, tired, & crimson.

The ticking of the watch is erotic beneath
this abyss of sky. silhouetting the black wings
of desire. This wind which sets the leaves
to trembling. The weight of dawn lifts itself
from our shoulders; we turn in our sleep, flutter our
hands, eyelids like stones; we will not wake.

naked as a fish among rocks & improbable trees
suffering a lucid mind. tears & leaves falling
the truth of a turning need. my broken pride rolls
on as a frustrated rage. breast soft, swallow high
she is thin as the rose which died the next day.

I was not kind to butterflies but to my garden.
you brush against my body; I break into a sweat.
this ache of noticing is an awesome weight.
is it a shameful sickness this loping desire?

Health Department lady knows what she knows
rattles her bracelets. levels her eyes:

Lady in the red dress, red heels
        come to talk about drug babies
        coke babies, moms with dirty urine
        roll their eyes, shows us the skinny
        'bout what shakes where all those
        sideways steppers got the addiction
        got that thirsty fire in their blood
        give it right to them innocent
        conceptions slowly spinning in their bellies.
Lady in the red dress, red heels
        taking pictures to hardcore parent aides
        doing the cross-wired time
        talking media too skinny in their need
        making babies, little twisted sisters
        shadow children,   not quite bent
        enough to die. Not quite. not quiet.
        success is gonna be a problem.
Lady in the red dress say
        these drug babies are hitting our schools
        filling daycare centers with their troubles
        cat screech babies gonna bend the world
        skinny little bird leg mommas
        late again, late again.
Lady in the red dress say
        mom caught ten years in the
        multigenerational pit
        been to treatment five times
        jailed once, never married
        four kids in the state's custody
        pregnant now, & high sideways.

Lady in the red dress say
      mom caught the relapse from her man
      sold her methadone take home dose
      for coke, left her kid with a friend
      out underground on our sweet cruel streets.
      ain't been seen for days.
Lady in the red dress say
      there's hope.   there's programs.
      there's money to throw at the problems.
      there's hope.   mom just caught a bad weekend.
Lady in the red dress say
      the baby's cries are inconsolable
      the baby cries, fists, & cries.
Lady in the red dress knows her momma.

My resume recounts all the things I once was

The heron's cry turns to ice in the inner bay.
loons chuckle; the owls turn to sleep.
Dawn melts the sounds, frees them drop by drop.

sisters chatter & whisper in the kitchen
trapping winter weeds with fresh planted flowers.

the years keep between us.
I put the strangle hold on my job
lose interest in weekend sports. prefrontal
shock treatments returning as a preferred
and billable service.   etching our brain waves permanently.

I drink my coffee, catch the bus at 6:10 a.m.
tule grass remains resilient in the sparse meadow.
I'm scared, and plan to stay that way.

"those who must be watched are assigned to each other."

hunger. cold-paned, in the meadow of married sex.
she turns like a hundred mirrors: reversed
passion is impeccable. though the colors transmit need.

much of our lives recedes into the dark norhtwest
dreaming energy from the stars:
ripe with pain & gin, bitterness
opens and closes her hands.
her belly swollen with moonlight.

pressing the beads, pushing the button.
women, and the wrong ones. Bone-torquing fear.
sky. same sky. after pissing in the halls.
industrial strength whale songs on the radio.

we wait where it rests. in emptiness
even the pumpkins melt. *insouciance.*
sans soucie. but, I tell you,
desperately alive. the catfish swimming and singing.
cinnamons? the moon in an opposite direction?
of course it was. lodestone cold.
alive beyond all cunning compasses.
I want to suffer; I want to fall. Bite sugar.

A sawed off dudeen.

a cold exploring, imploring
hand upon the shivering breast. reluctant, cling
to bare. there's running flame in the trees
& frost at the eyes of morning. tomorrow.
snow or ice.

stark/empty/life?/maybe/but, not a game.
an unchained mouth. one more dental caries
& too many mirrors. the abrogation of it all.

spacing letter part doing the dozens down on the 'stablishment.
"once be all there is." there is a wave;
there is an omen, awesome, the trees take off their
leaves. leave taking metempsychosis. soil naked
with life clutching down. the dark edges darken.

stomach filled with flames, fire.
Trapped in the comet's flowing hair is the answer.
an utter hive of stars.

"have Proton, Mutual Pneum, " will travel.
can gear infinite to nuclear & time to space.
the swinging of the pudendum, into matter or what
doesn't. light curves back around.

There are many ways of being led by the nose.
the comforter will not come; there are no such signs.
nobody has to surrender.
though what can be taken, is taken.
after midnight, even the dolls go whoring.

transcendensity!

the hush of imbalance.
all the airport visionaries gathering
for one last layover.
all peppered with inertia
& spice.

the mice are growing teflon.
the hands fall through.
these celestial guitars of echo.

murmur up murmur down
mother dream rocking
night draws the last boats
in chalk pastel, home to the island.
" . . . taking friends to bed
for warmth we no longer feel from mates."
As soon as you quantify
"random" it isn't anymore.

There we wuz noshing hors d'oeuvres when . . .

Dylan Thomas dead of "alcoholic insult to the brain."
His best friends claimed the US killed him.
the children rabble together. a bawd & a virago??
the streets are up to no good. prescription bottles
and wine empty. The street empties them out.
back when the maples were burning
the weather was bad; the sky ugly as
beer which abolishes all grief.

If we ever get to heaven
we'll have to help with the thunder.
the doctor is the coffin nail.
the misery index is the sum of unemployment rate
& rate of poverty. why ask this indicator
living on Imperial squeezings and cheap wine?

Roots of dogwood (tea), not bark, for
quinine (fever) (malaria & sweat)
"because animals are so dark
        & they move so fast
        they absorb almost all the light
                that you throw at them."

generally helpless on the page

the hands like milk through the air
the will swims like iron. He had
a callous on his character.

beauty & roses blooming—turning the burdens
of anorexia, beads of unworthiness counting
the sky a blue shout of sky. memory the
mother of nine. in an empty boat.
"palimpsests of sand" blue star in blue
sky. where? salmon: roe & melt in a redd:
black-eyed alevin yolk sacs, fry, parr
smolt, shakers, bright, glossy, then dull
& hook-jawed, long-toothed, fasting to spawn.
a man wishing to lead elves in a song.
spawned out, dull, murky, flesh falls away
the circle of water filled with life.

the sun drifts toward raw meat, raw heat of
blistered vision. puddles of rotting carp.
Dead, she left a mound of salt, small
mound. plowing the mice into the field.
count long enough & history will break
off. even the shadows will not lie down.
that light here right now. the ambition
of water is at least level. though not
still. The wind is a dry thirst of
air. acorn brown breasts. burning in the creek
stars catching light on the water.

it will be spring & the crickets will count faster
from their rock burrowed sleep. it is their
special mercy not to wake. pride complete of
itself. "booze, lies and mercy."
here in the nidus.
"You can drink an ugly girl pretty
  But you can't drink a fat girl thin."

"dog food," she said.

loved beyond the fade, jaded not may be
deepest rich wine, the stars lost grace
and gained a marble heart. loveless in a weeping
land, sordid & weary. forest & river.

when she screams blood the front steps are stained;
the stairwells stream, and the back porch steams.
fire forms flowing flowering furious waterfalls
he took shy of a sudden on some when drunk on bliss
there is no clear inkwell of night.
"Sirius, Betelgeuse, and Procyon"
the brightest of Orion's bindlestiff.

"What can make the heart ache more than a billboard?"
the fish do not tremble before the tides.
nor the birds before the wind.
Fish so thick they make the water shine & glint like stars.
entesselate the willow wrings her weeping hands.
rich in poverty and diamonds of dew.

Kimboed

lisp & purl. twirl & gleam. sent out of dreams . . .
mad lips smothered whisper
his mind, though dull, was notched like a saw.
silence thundering till daylight/till dawn eats away
the transparency of gin. lonesomely piping of gulls.
the splendor of their slender voices. and their stories on
whistling voices. mortified granite

he rinsed his eyes in wine
but his sight did not clear. wizened, hideous.
faded: life is the cage – we beat the bars.

"The trouble with poetry is
that it's too exhalted."
"We are living in a pygmy day."

the tangle of his wild eyes and hair. out
on the jetty wind; the skies are still & dark
& late & singing. "gay-like
& crazy with the blues." ideas haunt him.
He dreams & pretends to fish.
time lags. Space falters.
dikes of stone. cowled sky.

FOUR VIEWS OF THE DESERT
from Charles Baudelaire

Our Ennui

Even in an artificial paradise, you can
escape from reality, but still have to come
back to get a good steak, even a free meal
at the mission or the soup kitchen.
On the streets Ennui smokes a houka or a
glass crack pipe. the froth of hatred,
a jaded eye. drunk and exhausted from
genuflections. prayers. hunger.
eyes still quaking with the night's visions.

wine shrinking the liquid sky, the useless stars.
black battalions, merged shades of grey,
walking tatters, alive still.

unfortunately, those lovely breasts no longer
guard a heart. sparks & blood, steel-grey eyes.
in his trembling need she saw a fix.
It was not a healthy fever.

These strange flowers, a curtain of shadow,
resentment & desire/ice & flame.

Time wins by law. A city changes as fast
as a young girl's heart. Rock-hard memories, heavy.
puny crack cocaine babies withering like bad flowers
in a cat-screech cry, totally inconsolable.

Her Ennui

Too new and young and strung on the excitement,
the lie of freedom, the lure of late nights
and independence. a sweet street flower in a profound solitude.
gleaming weapons. not quite pendulous
breasts. the innocence & sweetness of first promises.

a world of metal & concrete.
a world of asphalt & steel. perfumed
like a hell's canyon wind. sage & sweet water
in a storm at night. she seeks
"a world less hideous; minutes less leaden."

long eyes, she had long deep eyes.
jealousy lined with suspicion and
indolence, like rain, cold as the moon
silent of its own accord.

magic sparks click from her pantyhose;
gold dust-like dandruff or the dead calm
of despair. the half-starved cry of night things.
lust turning itself over in sleep
like a wanton philosopher dreaming alchemy.

she had eyes so wicked that no one believed her begging.
A look that could sharpen an icecube.
half open, her robe, her great coat.
her bed was deep as the grave & the sheets all stained.

His Ennui

he was charged with nonchalance. easy solutions.
Like a wind from Havana, musky. "night street:
gold, steel, light & diamonds." all the glitter outside.

hatred, no matter how drunken, does not
pass out and sleep beneath the table. Oh, he can
laugh, but he simply cannot smile.
phosphorescent eyes. each lost second cuts
a bit of pleasure into lost, also.

As mad now as in the past. Heaven or hell
at least it will be new. She turned
with her terrible hand, eyes ablaze
with the hatred which makes anyone fight.
her dreams reflected hell. nixies & pixies.
rhetoric and satan caught in the staircase
of the County/City Building.

vertigo. vertiginous: nonchalant be a smooth
& troubling way of living. she bends over
her breasts and his brain catches fire. And
he will sob like a fountain of water blessing the night.
Street evil and skanky, like, off and gone too long.

Their Ennui

the homeless
multiply themselves against the woe of the streets.
iniquity. inequity. honey for sorrow, religion
for no other options left. bare feet and a bloody spade,
the work nearly done. a sweet savage sorrow
alone on the streets. and empty. missing
the sweetness of a home they never quite lived.

Hell-born, hell borne, & hell-born again. & borne again
and again. irony & insanity,
they find equilibrium in words.

Flame-filled eyes, the thousand-yard stares.
loose on the cruelest local streets.
All clocks are brutal in the misted Monday morning.
Wine, like a tomb wraps you warm, dulls the pain.
From our love is born poetry and poverty:
"God created sleep; Man added wine."

Masked in a shroud of wine, Pride makes us equal to god.
The blue crystal of morning cannot philtre
last night's tome-filled edges, cool as all things break
to man's sore touch. drunk on the wind
& the howl of the storm, an angel would
damn himself for her. even the wind is changeable.
The summer ends and the street looks long.

Island of Destiny

unbuilding the bone. remembering

crossing horse heaven hills
star frost folded deep against the dark side
of the treeless hills.

the mountains belong to no one.
the streets belong, depending
on the time of day, to the tired,
the hungry, the cold stoned, the cops,
the dead. the country here is hungry;
the sun bleaching moisture from the shadows.

Time gives up only waiting.
city discipline washed out
of his hair by the wind
each ferry home to the island.

old stories walking in their own tattered sleep.
the sea breaking its toys on the beach
casting them off among the rocks.
and he breaks his body against the long commute.

she had a grindstone of a heart
stone to sharpen any good cold steel.
the quilt of skin, the skein of hair
even his brain danced widdershins.

Following the Equinox
for Octavio Paz

silvestre = savage (think of this when you see tweety)

resting in a strange calmness, dancing inside
heron's wings unfolding the sky. The noise of
workmen on the street turns out to be the
pileated woodpecker saving for winter as the
light is pecked away by the shortening sun
its course on a diet of sky diaphanous.

I'm on you like ivy climbs the fir & maple trees.
she wears a skirt of rising tide.
memory is the path to an empty room.

hair done up by a tumult of spiders & that
inquisitive woman at the beauty parlor
the thin one, her shadow as long as autumn.
Each curl a question in her breath.

"I do not write to kill time
nor to revive it
I write that I may live and be revived,"

ashes, dust, & dirt in love, profoundly in love
& lost in the desire to forget death, gravity, & time.
does my memory yet burn in your body?

The breaker wave-crashing sound of the freeway
throbbing in my temples.   her name is high tide
in a small sheltered harbor. clawed lightning
scratched across the sky. her knees half open
she drinks her lazy coffee, adjusts her skirt
turns back to her desk. it is her legs that draw
my eyes. "the mouth of moss." nakedness is ancient.

"every poem is time, and burns. . ."
cutting the brambles by hand. Listen, inside this
little nested paper ball of hive, the wasps debate.
this woman, wasp waisted, a desire each night
breasts which burn like morning. Yesterday the
sky was unanimously blue. Cutthroat trout clear the
water, leap & arc through the air without a thought.

Two trees were felled to make way for the road;
those remaining whisper & lean together.
the land slips into its dreaming after the equinox
mendicant moon of September. hunger or drugs
among the wind-mangled clouds, it is the
passion of insects, the intelligence of the ants
or the bees. We plant our passion
like a tree, it grows slowly steadily at
first, but it grows. The tide wanders like
lost syllables, extra syllables, around the island.
the birds settle down among the branches &
the trees lean into the darkness. The birds
mutter the terror of last winter's frozen starvation
they recount their losses. Tracking the footprints
of each lazy afternoon in which there was less song.

"You were born to live on an island"
my eyes wash under your clothing pale darkness
a fever quickness catches fire to your clothes
& even your shadow burns. He paces the water
in chains, the birds in a dry land, and you, he
prefers naked. shadow skin, cinnabar lips
the tall cedar, thin tree chained by the wind
feathered limbs murmuring of the coming winter. Gathering
the sky to the windows in a fountain of fading time

"Poetry,
suspension bridge between history
and truth."

"the island of her breasts"
the horizon is liquid, the pulse, your
blood's footsteps.

Thought is a liquid flame which murmurs
against the raindrops. a tapestry of foliage.
Look to Tacoma across the troubled waters;
the lights glimmer, shimmer. His eyes were
thirsty; his hands lacked respect. He drank
her breasts, pawed at her thighs, cupped her small
breasts in his glass of scotch. sculpts a short
future of fantasy & whispers, desire turning
in the swirled ice, the smoky barroom. Fingertips
like small eyes, clarity cages the new day with
something it must mean.   the sun nestled among
the three sister fir trees.

Ground glass to dogs while the painted smiles
persist among the bastioned brotherhood. Waiting
outside locked doors for the Health Board to deny
their raises in executive session while the rain
teaches us patience. waking to the must of each
morning. life as a fragment of time, a function of
gravity and the need of water to move. viewing
history as punishment.

drifting among the evolutions of ferns
& brambles, time in motion. Time passes
& gravity stays; motion neither passes nor stays.

A house with walls of water waiting for life
beneath the bridge. magnetism draws us into
closer, tighter circles. Stretching to meet the
shadow of my words. The mercy of time is that
it does go by, & it doesn't really seem to come back.

presiding over a government of birds.   unbreakable
air chain: inspired, expired, held only for a slow
blood beating moment of time.   avoiding the blade of
war — the hurting words—the bitter food of conflict.
Burning lamp in an empty room.   Time to plant the
Winter-sleeping bulbs, nestle them in darkness'
moist island earth, air, & future of spring sun.

Fire & foliage, they wake to the traffic, shake their
chains to clear their worn eyes.   Move from the
Mission, the Last Chance Shelter, from street corner
to street corner watching the clock strike no truce
merciless among the wasted dizziness of dying
having given up already, there are in butterflies
downtown.   Large star, crescent moon, enormous
distance from here to town.   sometimes my
words drink me in; sometimes they spit me out.
smaller growing moon too new & this star escort
the night as it empties out.

crossing the street, standing on corners for no
good reasons the horizon blurs. venus anchors
the sky. No moon this morning & the night empty.
most confusions are stubborn as my blackberries'
persistence. Dancing & flourishing in the rain
yet to come. The memories of an old woman mist
the windows. weeping down to the sill
nude descending a stone staircase,
the cold poverty of November
inching toward us in the recession. the cemeteries
fill with names. The lines of unemployment lengthen.
The small tribes of crows prepare for winter
preening the sidewalks for whatever's there.

wavering between doubt & faith drinking the rain
if the sun lives more in the west, why does it die there?
when the gods do not speak their games are terrifying.
Does a dream have weight? is emptiness weight?
When do my eyes become souls? constellations erased
by dawn. prayers with no lips, no sound. like sand at
a long distance collapses. each instant opens then
closes past me. all hours empty out; they can
hold no sand. The death which wants me knows
my place already. all faces are in the face of the dead.

the tide at rest nearly turns to stone. The dust of
present/current sources is sleep. rain washes its bare feet
To read is a fragile suspension of reality's reality.
each real soul is transparent. the sun is not relenting
neither is the wind, nor the rain, the frosted coldness.
mix night, water, music & electricity, receive a woman.

the fish's fin cutting the wake of water in the
Hell's Canyon moonlight. flaming water/rocky air.
inventing each thing. each reality in each new day.
Opening the doors of the morning. closing the windows
of night. The hours are blades, the minutes' flakes
of obsidian, the seconds flow by. Coyote
interrogating the moon, questioning why.
image of a catfish traced in the stars.

the hand that writes is stubborn. baits its own
hooks. Time is a seed which sleeps in our heads.
hours falling into the sand. Toe numbed by
needles excising the root of the nail. mind
falling like a stone returning to the beginning
lighting the shadowy corners filled with whispers.

The frogs reach out to us in the afternoon calling
from the creek bed, from the spring, calling to us in
this late & warm October.   collected by summer
& left for the fall. each moment becoming
more & more enormous. Crossing the shining asphalt
Crossing the traffic void.   Crossing the trust of
street logic: waves, water, flame, air. your fingers
crossed also.   Placing your shadow on this page.
To explore the valleys & plains of your body
in the dawn.

The old wind rustles my memory; the sun clears my
eyes. resting in the black water of your sighs.
time traced as fate & work in your hands.
A changeling left out of the tide of desire
struggling through uncertain territory, precarious,
near the fall, the falling edge. an afternoon burning
as I turn myself to a whisper, a puff of brief smoke.
rage & holiness; respect & duty; pleasure & desire
knotted together in the flesh, dependent upon breath.
Life is a wound without healing today. the worm's
been gnawing at our bodies, sending them towards
constellations.   stillness in our eyes. learning the
timeless art of dying, inventing our own Edens
over & again.   "Touch the leaf, and the tree trembles."

neither love nor longing
for Herman Hesse

the old shoes have gathered god into them
& the wind finds no home at all. The leaves of yellowed
fall begin their laughing, knowing all winters are
far far away. The night falls into us also
& the city streets across which the leaves skitter
are small & moving to ruins. The poor long for
stars & moonlit nights. dream in their pain
for stumbling relief, such fierce irreverent dancing.

longing has no future but its own secret love.
There is no reason why the mountains huddle
together outside the limits of the city, its breathing
passion. the sorrow of an echo. a song caught
in the throat – clutched in delicate hands
each night bound to come; each morning
intricately chained, chained to your strange hands.

there is absolutely no way to keep the time from
coming. there are no paths back, & we are lucky
for this fact. the moth's wings fan the flames
homesick forever. arrival as empty as departure
the traveling dream. days of heavy fire, red sweet clover.
too bitter to be alone. silence darkens the memory
of your hair, the paths confused. distance is
silent only for a moment. the sky is weeping time.

Practicing The Yoga of Pain

A child's right hand found floating
in a manmade lake in a north-end
suburb of Tacoma. They sent in divers
a child's small right hand
And no reports of still children missing
a child's small right hand
They found nothing else
a child's small right hand
Tomorrow officials will drain the lake.

Tomorrow I will ride an early bus
and go to this town Tacoma
the long hard way by ferry to Seattle
& I will wait for buses in the rain
& I will get to work a bit too late
& I will tell my stories of broken ferries
on the Point Defiance Talequah run
turn on my computer, check my mail
through cups of coffee black & all day
I will try to forget over and over
a child's small right hand.

Rimbaud Left Uncollected

suffering and pleasure; black moons, white moons,
pub crawling, then tobacco, hashish, opium:
Verlaine shoots him in the wrist; two shots,
one missed.   at 37, the most random number.
a man "damned by the rainbow," he's on strike
disordering most of his most frail sensibilities

The writing of rhymed prose!
the soul made monstrous suffering & madness
an enormous normal precurser of action
poetry ahead of action, leading the action,
leading to action. This crowding together of the
heart,   the birds of autumn, the unanimity of their flight
numb wings – grey skies.

a shivering song which chants its measure
with shining hair & tangled eyes we wake with
the angel which guards our slumber. we are springtime
drunk with sunlight beneath a sky too small
covering beneath doubt's wings, shivering at the edge
of the waves. black moss between her thighs. each
thigh smooth as a slumbering alder. melting towards
him. they grin at the sky, this dark combat of love.
breaking fingers on the streets, breaking heads in court.
sweet fearsome woods dumb with love & bleeding.

brutal desire's as necessary as breathing, thoughts
a swirl of mad kisses, a rose that lived one night &
withered & died in the morning light. She kissed me
like a crazy spider. planting trees among the uncertain
foliage. Frogs piping from the brackish creek water.
Here so long sometimes that I feel myself growing
into my furniture; everything the same wood-grained
grey. darkness nosing the edges of the creek like
an angel nuzzling the back door of an uptown bar.
toying with the dreams of heaven wishing to lie
among the irises, the wild flags
looking to heaven and sweating with obedience.

the wallpaper mildewed, the room filled with distractions
strange shawls of moldy fabric wrapped/draped about
the cheated beating hearts.

Longing for the tawny breath of spring in this city
which knows painfully that it will always be number two.
trusting only in the weaver's unclouded love.
she dips her hands into the moonlight
giving me, lending me strength to turn
& face the ugliness of this world in silence
so profound I can hear the beating of your eyelashes.
The winter comes clenching the fist of the city.

beneath a coraled archipelago of stars
from this island earth glimpsed only slightly
through the hovering jostling clouds of the full rains
the dawn is heartbreaking; the moon-bright path
broken by clouds. the owls are restless. calling
from the dying maple by the beach, calling from
Margery's woods, from the last few standing firs.
These conniveries of language lost to France.

the north wind spares not a leaf and the leaves
of the willows pale, yellow, & fall. The man has no
reflection on waters rough as these. The sound of rocks
crackling together – the sound of angel's singing the
complaints of angels. Here in the moon's cold sweat.
Venus, the sure sister of the blues. Patience dies happily.
a dream is pure loss; dawn scatters the scent of night.

The branches die their fainting dance in this
first freezing wind of winter/fall. watching the
relentless seasons wear me out.

the early morning avenue is cold & vacant.
the black hair of morning is a fit of hunger.
Old Rimbaud called the skunk the Rocky Mountain cat.

a prayer to the rainbow across a desert of marjoram
& thyme her eyes turned gently unhappy.
the lights of the city are an enormous distance.
"even great music falls short of our desire."
the colors deepen & detach themselves.
she shudders and the world sings now in black & white.
running to the stupor which awaits me. a harsh sky
an angry biting, nipping, tearing wind.   hashhish
assassin.   the sky rings down like grey crystal
frost on the docks, the tide low, the mountain
capped with a mushroom cloud, the sun grey rose
rising as people with no need to know each other fill
the city, pass each other every day – still say nothing.

this astonishing chicken, astonished chicken announcing
the dawn. the wine of the caravans, the mist of golden
hashhish.   even the dream has grown cold.
we are living in the exact middle of time(s). black desert
lulled by the rocking movement of the current.
Reality has its thorns; it bleeds also; tired wings
dragged through evening shadow; reality also flies.
fat as a fish & all lit up.   grinning like a clam.
standing in the radiance of virgin shadows.
the infliction of the moment & the infinity of mathematics
logic fully unexpected.

Staring out into the vast astral silence unmoved
under the cold influence of scenery the silent rage
of boredom.   Carbonic plague harries the city
a storm of drunkenness the mob has no integrity
understanding the bitterness of beauty . . .

"I called up executioners in order to bite
their gunbutts as I died."   A fine trick of madness
living at/on/out pot-sherds & nettles. idle & brutal
looking forward to a good drunken sleep on the beach.
chasing after satan's moonshine, paying the taxes later.
As a carnivore I bury the dead in my belly.
"I believe that I am in hell, therefor I am there."
"Hell cannot touch pagans –"
Standing among the voiceless trees, stranded among
the red alders of November; hallucinations of words

"the hedge spider eats nothing but violets,"
despite the lovely lonely night he stood among the
shadows & the whirlwinds of dried leaves.
grow fogs, eat fever, enough to give the dead bad dreams.
Venus, a silver star, traced in spiritual combat.
He looked; he thought and lived the dream.
He looked and finally turned around
He looked and walked away, thoroughly modern.

ankle deep in grass the star shower falls
& unafraid she walks unafraid with her hair
well down, undone, the earth bent dawn once more.
Dead winter waiting for April's sheen.

& there the old fence was
briar tangled & whimpering in the wind.
the luminous arpeggio of her fluttered
bird-like hands.   tender words often will
not prevail.   this woman speaks of bees,
wild, gentle, flowers over and over again.
must be a gardener. dawn broke in her
heart & there were tears and flowers.

Trees are Tangled

Tangled up in blue

& god created blue to define the edges
of the land: sea & sky.   Life & breath framed
in blue, living in winter knowing shades of grey
drying into blue & the sky does not open.

smothered every working day by mediocrity
though the trees are tangled in the sky
god has a green thumb, is more ancient than
shadows. a regular, everyday, fragile wonder.

blue teaches the stones envy, gives them weight.
white birch. blue sky. no shadows. mist beneath
the trees. tolerable. Imagine god with
a handful of seeds & dirt on his knees.

that first blue breath spinning in our dreams
opposing the habit of love
retouching the wounded heart
growing beyond blue

There is some obscure boiling anger in the privacy
of women. & seeing this anger is a kind of genius.
the constant insistence.

sadness swarms the marshy ground.
a lingering winter cloud hovers over the mouth
of Judd Creek.   Something there gone too cold
to freeze, too cold to tumble from the sky.

The sword of need rusts at my side
stone silence tumbles from the trees, dull leaves
the red surgeon's knife of dawn silence
unnerving the clouds. the young dreams
the melting touch on my neck.
The hush and roar of breakers miles to the coast
this fantasy of weariness blent with absence
of hope. a simple darkness
suspended in a quiet near warm rain.

"The crying business of the street"
calls me to work each standard day.
even the tired sweetness has packed and gone.
The crickets stir from their drowsing
become more remote.

Choose again;

we must always add to the healing of the world
vision = perceiving content instead of form.

burning body sugar with aerobics instead
of honest work. The moon climbing the sky in
some past life, a movie gone slow motion.

The wind blows rough & the house sighs.
The wind through the walls rustling her hair
in sleep. the shadows waffle & sigh.

Look at all the stars in the grass
this field of flooded sky. The stars breaking up on
the fallen waters' rippled surface. The prosecutor
permitted him to plead guilty. Night children.

I wish to die speaking to the Rotary Club.
can't keep nobody warm when you're dead, when
your breath stops. Learning the critters of the
neighborhood. Rocks may not be as beautiful as
flowers, but they last; they last forever.
In search of the mossy groin, the soft wonderful
place. An odd scent of burning. Drugs beading
in my veins. Justice allows, supports, reinforces.

working in the garlic fields of hell
learning to be alone in the house
too many voices giving advice in the blood-rimmed course
of the new year.   Nothing but bills in the mail
preferring the well-trimmed map to the edge of the woods.
preferring to run south with the sun
Television can't even numb these eyes.

I have not grown tired of this desire as you snip
the knots & slide. The strings that are left all
tangle together in this bitter winter wind.

Sometimes you're the enduring wave of my
salvation. sometimes it's just a fight.
Though the leaves outside are resting
our sedation, our slowness to move remains.
Still the glass is breaking. There are sharpened
edges everywhere. Whispers which we
refuse to share. The largest trees have
stumbled forward into the cyclone.
Their feet, somehow, gone to water or disgrace

Silence burns & smolders between our teeth.
The cats disappear; the birds scatter;
they rouse from their beds, & bound in flight,
they run,   simply "dreaming the house."

the "what ifs" color our conversations.
harbor-bound wind shakes the knob upon our doors.

Today. today, without hesitation
the storm has driven you into the yard.
"These doors are ours no more."
The griefs are old & arrive in details too
full & complete to have been real during
this. our life together.

refracted by her light, by her cold motion to leave
speaking to lawyers in the late morning
having endured the cyclone & burned our personal rage
the powers of electricity arriving too late now
for the south end of the island, here we are
squandering its darkness.

The days grow longer & you more cool & distant
dicing our extravagance into take & leave.
I have to leave the room, pretend to be asleep
to hear you laugh, so troubled by my touch.
still trying to say the unsaid, my bed is cold,
though half still mine. the deer bedded down
so they can look in the windows, rise but do not
run as I walk my way by for work.

our dreams turned only to facts of sweat, iron, & blood.
the tension of our middle years, years slipping
and comfortable, even in our arguments.
cold anger in the morning, nothing can breathe
beneath our bed. The dance, it seems, is canceled.
Who would have thought ordinary happiness this difficult?

I can hardly wait to lie naked in a naked sun again
broken like a mirror with no legs & too much time
to fall.   the leaves & vines reach into the
room like the whispers of our past
outside growing through the windows.

each year may be a dungeon (with no key)

If we were quiet the stones would have to tell.
Insight fails – the coyote leaves his winding tracks
careless fifty yards from camp. These women receive
us & we fill them like a creek fills the Sound or
the tide musters change.   lucid drunkenness
with the conscience emptied & pure.   blazing polished
stone, a glint of water.   frustration brought him back.
the vague fragrance of past love which lingers on . . .

in the fields of blue morning, dozing heron edges water.
the sweet poverty of farm critters rolling their eyes
the indulgent arms of god & the swift angles of light
know the heron.   Sweet water in a dry camp
crossing & recrossing a mark of possession
these high airborne loopings; the calculus of women
all the areas beneath the curve.
the rough & steady virtue of mathematics.
a fingerprint traced in the sky,
wheeled flock of dark birds.
Now that they are gone, where are they?

Tend the flowers which bloom.
A slow code of openness this crowded calm of summer.
something made the forest sigh.

"Fragile Fox II to Fragile Fox I:
Do you read me?   Over."

the living accept simplicity;
on the dead it is imposed.

strings and a harp; rifles & bullets/cartridges.
each man's song travels.   don't walk on the trail.
death leaves no more questions in our eyes.
tsunami does not wait.   tatami does.
time turns to silt.

back with the thousand yard stare.   twilight.
one planet hovering near the horizon

standing stock still under a government issue moon.
so real even the smells came back – as memory
so real, so real.   the gonads march.
The tricks: heads up means heads down.
people and dreams: more dreams than people.
suicide sat up with him all night writing notes.
writing the same note.   Home from the goddamn war.

"The weaker the wine."

checkered shadows of a waning moon. the dust of the
dead & a moon toad. thick wine dispels cares.
into the night the tide rushes. the living are parted
the dead are gathered together. all lewd reports yearn
for the past. a wine cup full of the moon. the rain fell
like threads. threads of rain weaving a grey grey day.

"Wine is the best reward of merit."
we grew older and less strong.
for the most part: fish who learn a fear of man
do not return to warn the others. Chuang Tsu,
dreaming he is a butterfly or a man.

fog so soft/light that it could not injure you, of itself.
It remains our slow afternoon. Fortunately there
is much more than an hour between the dog & the wolf.
the air is not blue, nor the sky, nor the sea,
yet they seem to be. yet they are. Wind always
arrives. arrives always where it should be when it
is <u>needed</u>. we are, here, toys of the rain. just big toys.
benighted by our centered perceptions of ourselves in
this. in this hugeness of things.

the woods dissolving into darkness at the top of the hill
the morning to turn winter bright
morning-blue heron-light hovering on the Sound
The dreams of last night slide out my windows
noiselessly up the hill through the woods
& gather there beneath the cluster of firs
to await the sleep of dreams.

each night is a little winter's sleep
returning with a mouthful of nothingness
          difficult majesty moving out of the
shallow end of the year.   dawn broke
                    we swept it up
                    went back to bed.

reality ground by the mill of sound – the burning
roadways.   no blood stirs in the air
attempting to maintain a high degree of indifference
to the pain, hate, suspicion, poverty which
feeds my doubt of social service truth.
the center responds to no inner or outer change.

pause beneath the praying tree
     our existence is enough evidence
The blackberries & azaleas holding their
breathless buds among all of this tenderness.
wind through wings & the uncompromising crows
predictable black leather biker birds.
stars hung high, bright cold, insistent & naked
The light not only seems to have body, but gives
its body to the trees, the grass, the gladiolas.
The secrets of the heron & the flounder
accepting the necessary limits, the boundaries, easily.
living life all day long.   missing the sound of the loom.

revenge like a weight in the heart of steel
smart as sandstone the crows wave their
incantations from the fir trees.
"teflon heifers" grazing the acres of time.
the last moans of the buffalo float
across the plains outside of Omaha.

vanquished deities speckle the shoreline
the traces of the wolf melt back into the landscape
the fusion of water in air.   It rains, nearly ten days now
it rains.   mourning melody: gondolas & violins
a network of dreams & fitful sleep without breath.
into the eyes of the elders.   That thing which happened
yesterday, more distant than Appalachia or
the Black Hills. Yesterday's morning.

Deep river, deep night, entering the darkness with words
a reflection reversed upon the water
savoring the nightmare / after the wild ride
slit her throat & bleed; barbeque for breakfast.
Takes the edge off hunger & fear from your eyes.
Incessant, the image of you, your faint smile, returns.
Keeps returning.   Seeing through the clear haze which
rests calm always in the eyes of the blind.
"Mythology . . . an eternal habit of the spirit."

Being inevitable there is no worry in destiny.
Killing is an ancient habit much like dreaming.
Oblivion of which the universe is made shines blue.

The crow raves

(oh, no! I've ruined this, will, so?! which (wish).)

The crow raves outside my palace.
my palace, too, was once on wheels.
my palace, too, was once on wings.

The crow raves!
Tide out so far that I gained 2 ½ acres
of land.   This makes me rich!
But the tide comes back, eats
my barge – takes back the land
& gives the taxes back.

The crow raves!
Two exclamation points return!!
If has been, might be, could have been
The story of his life, but he let
everything happen.   Time exactly in front
of him.   (I've been in jams like that myself.)
Thank god (something)!   I'm only telling his story.

The crow raves!
Why is it getting cold?
why can't we turn this thing
around? Why does the Department
of Social & Health Services think that it
is an ocean liner? why do I
want to know? why are you here too?

The crow raves!
I wish I could remember to keep
my guard up and believe you.
This troubles me deeply as a day old rose.
why must there be only arms
full of one & the sway of time & gravity
& expectation?   Do you want to dance?
     Shall we dance?
There are many things the darkness cannot hold.

The crow raves!
picking the thorns from my hands
I can't leave till I leave tonight.   &
maybe I don't want to leave; maybe there are
otters in the creek; maybe there are
pileated woodpeckers cooing in the woods.
Just kind of keeping the trails open & complaining.

A Kind of Clear Negative

memory foreshortens all of the distances
hunting that tight knot of wanting
I dream that she cries in her sleep
wake with the salt taste of her at my lips.

the whole front yard filled with watery light
black flowers lining the house boards as
I shake this sleep
        this sleep from me
        myself from sleep.

images here keep repeating like anchors in the stream
the deep stream of word/fantasy
gives this some implied continuity
a where to hang our hats.
let the dawn thicken like milk
let it run flaming down the side of mountains
down mountainsides & fill my glassy eyes.
urgent, we move forward with hunger
& terrible.
making love: a kind of speech to prove
existence, a language of being.
a contact with/through other bodies.
moving the devastated earth. moving
love hiding crouching behind/within bodies
great trees swaying above the cool stone house.

some image clear on the negative
where wind has brushed.
gothic clouds & shredded branches at the moon.
the air shaking with light
with her longing hair she comes tolling
& one single shadow blankets it all.

some sameness exact & nearly named
some wheel turning backwards, or seeming to
with the light & its pure
circular speed about the center.
a true tin angel on a stick,
her own voyeur until she dies.

Sprinkling blossoms on the floor

out near the fog hung creek the trees lean forever
into coming past.   each day beneath the shroud
of dawn they wait for healing, patient as their
leaves color & fall.   patient as the island's red tide
windless & quiet.   The leaves are laughing all over
the island, all over town.   the swallows having
been flocked again and gone for weeks.

you will not forget these eyes,   the cold bite of the coming wind.
the desperate blankness of the waiting fog.

sprinkling lavender blossoms on the hospital room floor
so the lavender rises for all who walk here.
lavender dried & crushed to rise healing through the air
the fragrance of lavender time lost in the healing
hospital trance.   time gone into the anaesthetized beyond.
& the faithful present heart.   this circle of concern
as I am washed between this walking dream and sleep.
dream strung memory of eyes.   the stir & sweet of fever's sleep
too far from the Sound to see the tide, all day from death
receding – all night from dawn retreating.
even the pain crosses over, a thousand yard stare
feeling tired & so very far away: October cold rain & grey.

the moonlight falls across, inch by inch, across the floor.
here in the city it's searchlights instead of stars
& sirens instead of nightbird sounds – the heron
startled from his reverie of fish & concentration.
a hungry memory which never sleeps, though the hours slide away.
and he does not forget.   forgets no hour, not one
past fish while the moonlight crawls till dawn.

thunder frozen in my heart, starlight gone brittle
& wavering. even for the blackberries the memory of summer
is growing old & spring is some pure far dream.
there is a secret strength in the island & always the
lonely bird-borne cry of dawn, a cup of anguish for the heart.
trembling, whispering bright magic moon & planet star.
the always rain.   moon & star & rain & distance the same.

The crows remain & my illness too passes away
The spike of fever weaker each cycle down
The sound breaks against the island
The salt diluted by the soft mouth of my creek
The geese exercising the endless vee of their daily flights
There is spring & lavender in my eyes. I heal
The wilderness returns. A tree's shadow broken by the wind.

lonelily at dawn the owl whimpers his territorial imperative
the moon & its star turn only to listen as
the crushed mint blows through my windows in the dusk.
crows have brave hearts, fear nothing in a flock, in murder
they fear nothing but perhaps the owl, & this only
when they are alone & near the dark of sleep.

The Unemployment Line on Venus

The unemployment line on Venus starts before the sun
runs all year seven days a week, twenty-four hours a day.
Lines looped halfway round the block
each person creature sweetly aware of their place in line.
Proxemics: real & regular. All spaces between are equal.
First come, first served.   Arrange yourselves like cattle.
The expressions are all the same, bored, patient, hopeless, ennui.
They make it hard to get what's coming to each of us
depressed beneath a greening sky.
The doors will open soon & we'll snake in behind security.

The unemployment line on Venus circles the heart.
Fills the downtown office with hopeful despair.
Can't win for losing. The name, the number, a computer error.
The waiting, the contacts, the social security number,
mental desolation. There must be something wrong with each of us.

The unemployment line on Venus wrings its many hands
against the cold dark hopeful morning. Fragile dreams
winding the crowd control barriers. No jobs in the morning
paper. The wrong form filled out completely
thoroughly circle back to the end of the line.
They've been open twenty minutes; now they turn
the person creatures away. The sparks are going out.
The fire's dying down. No jobs here. No hope here.
Compassionate like the unemployment line on Venus
bats its eyes, "come back tomorrow."
Where the sparks circle and dance.
The extinct creatures return to wait.
& the green fires the sky gone luminescent.
The unemployment line on Venus rivers on
followed through this low downtown by twilight.

The unemployment line on Venus has no shadows
because each one in it becomes a shadow.
Line up here enough times & even your pride &
what's left of it disappears. But the line holds.
Not even a shadow of these shadows standing in the line
waiting in this unemployment line on Venus.

This can't be the earth, this city, downtown, the City
of Destiny. These are only shadows. This can't be the earth
the sky is not right, but this is the only line in town.
The bureaucracy is not, has never been, modest.
If this is how it is. If this is our destiny. Then we want another
line. (We want something quite else.) in which
we can cast our own shadows. Without this waiting line
we want our shadows back.

Left carrying ice to an argument

sweating death like a sentimental orgasm
a selfsame joyous anger. still here.
the barren clearcut eroding pale salmon
nothing to still the lash of the rain.
nothing will absorb & retain. the ensemble
of trout gill gasping in the turgid runoff.
heart beats more faint each muddled
winter, each waterless summer. the cries in the
clearcuts wandering away without echo.

Time unfolds, immediate, tree flesh in the sheeting rain,
thorn berries drooping green, ripening towards long days.
a cloud mad rush takes the sky. free of intention though
bound firmly somewhere. the chainsaws finally masturbating
clear-eyed loggers in the unemployment line.

you have gone like the light upon the water, blinked away
the dawn has been arrested for breaking too early.
the wild heart rhythm measuring bright sustenance
junked out on technocracy, rushing onward for more and more.
the streets & trails gone ageless & nonlinear.

each evening the children throw off their greyness
each morning they put it on like a translucent
promise. here we stand at the muzzle end of culture.

her hair flames in my hands. the smoke of destiny
quick to heal; quick to forget, yet insisting on wilderness.
a barbarous world view. full circle, waking world
creeping toward the indefinite edge of dawn.
the dampness hidden is me calling you still
the musk of petals fondled by spring rain.
the haiku of her walking, my compulsive consumption.

formaldehyde of hope to save it for tomorrow
steak & saddle shoes of the past; gene mutations
mutating the mushroom clouds, the oil slicks
making finer & finer ashes of the dead. war a
word of fire – a world of fire. An unforgettable fire
skin smooth as a far blue sky. arsenals,
armaments, & ashes. A bow on a saw wishful
thin, poor & weary. A thermal pulse. A wave of disaster
stockpiling devastation. Leaves come with instructions
to fall. thermonuclear ovens, clouds, mushrooms.

world go boom. the sleepers waking from their rubbish
smiles exchanged like business cards or utility bills
tossed water, splash of a laugh. sky opens like a
big blue door & the sun falls through, & the heat falls down,
when she breathes in my mouth, the ashes stir & glow
strike fire.

The deadly birds of the soul are caught in the lights.

the days keep stacking against us
while you have been gone I have grown much older
& my heart did not break, but turned to stone.
I have forgotten how to be lost, how to find my way.
I remain, not innocent, but still a trembling fact.

The eagle at the mouth of the creek perches & eats
the bird which didn't pay enough attention to the sky.
In the city the skin toughens up—you don't want
to go up to Twenty-third. In the middle of the
Ave. they shot her—in the middle of the Ave.
She died. Those Spanish apartments up on Portland
Ave? You don't want to go there either. Blue to
love blue. As if we were gods the wind touches
us & in the right colors we own the street.
& the big dark bird is only a shadow
in the street lights. the angels are doomed.

Though trees are tangled in the light innocently
it seems all beyond saving.
Left only the smoldering bits of a dream navigating
in the darkness. daily striking words into song.
death is a dark plum which the tree is ripening
every green journey has its beginnings, leaves stretching
to sun. each of us a fugitive, then refugee, then vagrant
finally completely alone with our quiet hands folded.
peacefully solving the riddle. nomads no more. for a moment
each of our bodies pausing —stopping at a mossy place.
a cup of rain. water hanging/draping flesh upon bone.

the geese fly by my bed each new morning, two voices
one shadow between them. twisting the misty bait of
memory until the moon is constant & pure.
Fear is always simple; unnamed things are more complex.
standing in the center of a circle waiting for someone else
to find us. the loss of innocence has nothing to do with sex.
it is much more terrible & persistent surviving our lives
navigating the darkness which remains.
only grief singing. our turning selves getting damn seldom.
dead of hope. empty of innocence.
what has happened? whose children have we become?
what can a new morning heal?

Stars Tumble Out

"ruing alien firmaments"

when the lines seem blurred I check my eyes
this year, the dogwood doesn't bloom; it's not my eyes
but some mycotic disease, only leafy shadows now
on the old garden, & brambles blackberry doubling
their time. The Sound, the rivers, Judd Creek, these all
find time. Lost in these "eagle ferns, " not even
knowing their common names. ripe blackberries &
rain is all the glory my heart can hold
reflected light, love wins its own silences
Fresh as the new wash drying on the line.

Sunset feeds the hungry heart, one prayer till morning.
trees grow nearer in the night.
shadows lurk with every light.
distance swallowed by foggy mist, a grey shawl of mist
moon borne & seeping down the alleys from the park.
The few remaining firs keep their secrets in the night
above these weary violent streets which once were
winding paths. They shade these frail young deaths.

"All are bound into a uniform edition, one can't be redeemed
by any of it anymore, only darkness and truth can do that now"
John Ashbery

Do the clouds imagine us? the winter does.
the storms wear us down. The wind knocks the petals
from the plum and cherry trees. resigned to no fruit
wearing the ashes of roses with a wearying sun
Asking favors of the fish with our weighted lines
the fish reading my poem backwards on the water.

seeking a way right back onto the conveyor belt
the story winds down. the shadows vanish
there is no protection, no guarantee that our sensibilities
will not haul us away. My friends watch the city
waken, the sun rise, the lights twinkle out across the
Sound from their pink-tinted room through glass.
Once we realize it we marvel at our own emptiness.
absence, being perfect, is difficult to measure, to
mold, to suffer. like my little cat chasing the shadow
of this pen: each time she catches it, it covers her paws.

the landscape here is longer than the city
& the weather always makes the first move.
the dream gains substance as I talk in my sleep.
each storm keeps its own secrets, tells of the others.
mystery and death are never the way we like it /them.
this may be the wrong dream, but it's too late to refinance.
Don't worry; it's stranger & more dangerous somewhere else.
It's a matter of getting home safe with a dream tonight
washing the tentacles of rain. definition is cruel;
take my hand. we have not been spared, though there is sleep.
the unused situations are still waiting in line. life cannot
be the same; something is always leaving.
the angels wear old tattered clothing, have no genitalia.
the clothes fit. when the wind stops they are trapped
in the branches of the fir trees. hungry &
ragged as crows & just as godless. each dream settles
for another smaller dream. mishandling the skein of time.

the tide gleans the shoreline for miles. thousands of them.
beauty finally leaves the eye of the beholder.
the casual chambers of your voice fail to warm me.
the year shambles into spring, and it has been a bear of a year.
children die in the streets, ice cream cone in one hand, cocaine
or a pistol in the other. they find themselves forgotten.
regret frosts our glasses. the ice cubes clink.
star-struck magnitude: the police return the fire.

"twist & trout on salmon chanted evening"

it's a short walk from breakfast to madness
eyeing the possibilities of lunch—the injections
or electroshock. Homeless in the institution
each of a kind, singular, & lost from family to the street.

Night mind & daylight eyes afraid to open.
Find yourself once again at 23rd & Ainsworth
where strange things are real & the cops' hesitation
is untold. the gulls still stitch the sky; pigeons
dodge traffic; & the peregrine falcon shows up for tv at
the Sheraton. you drive the blocks with your hunger
stealing mine. leaving a song that remembers on the beat
the heart beat—the driving end of sex—the swimming into
darkness. this is not dancing. Cindy, the good elephant,
now she knows dancing & the burst of the trainer's ribs.
The sound of bells & flight. the ring of danger in each night.
From which you'll never die of cancer waiting just to live
knowing history as a guess, something done which you might
have said. brushing the new dark which tugs life from
our eyes. leaves us quaking ashamed to die.

dining on elves & trout flies, chips of moonlight falling
on the water. Sinking under water will not put out the sound.
My little cat is dreaming she runs & smurrs in my lap.
outside the green chanting of the blackberries & the grass
breaks the sky into raindrops, like a grey breath in my hair.
a grim & predatory day, I turn into someone going home.
in the rain, the streets hissing under stray Friday tires.
you are a bright stone in my hands, heavy, brilliant & river
rounded. an anchor in this streaming falling mist.
My lawn fills with the gold of lion's teeth—my hillside with
nettle & berry vines, brambles & sweet fruit. There is sweaty
work to do as the dreary weekend comes. I will bleed.

having gone finally south
for margareta waterman

a book which is whispered. new rhythms once again in a
purple shirt. bleeding out our lives on the crowded
streets — in our lonely rooms. none of us can resist looking
it's why she didn't come back. like familiar dancers
melting together into the rhythm & the pattern.
looking through the mirror, not at it. you have to
keep walking, even after you find the answer.
the seeds hold their breath; the bulbs soften & flex for spring.
love draws the eyes open. tangles the feet & the wind
in glandular reasons. clouds soaring over the city
cold in april, avoiding mirrors, searching for sweet berries.
the rain will not wash it away. we're shooting through the
stars, even if we aren't shooting for them.
each of us just another dancer in the starlight—in the
dancing in the shadows —shadows.

In the crosshairs
for Marion Kimes

the balm of the cello in this chanted voice
the disarray of grey skies against the burning coal of
being something alive & walking. breathing beneath this sky
parallel circuitry. the clock's face is a page of hours
trapping the nonsense of promises, these disappointments
which are real & may not be confined in words or pages.
in these oceans of possibilities. liquid languid
eyes, the smooth beckoning of sockets of their thighs
women gone all beautiful below the equator.
innocence & suffering in these long long days.
the raggedy ann wind rumpling my thinning hair.
the ongoing compromise of life turning us, changing.
there is nothing chivalrous about fire or the mists
of what we do not know. this animal which will not
move. will not relent.

Hanging out down to Dead Puppy Beach

life is but a falling leaf. whose catspaw are we?
cats insinuate themselves among my books & shelves
among the gladiolas & dahlias. hanging out all night
along the little path through the woods. a tortoise shell
wight. a scampering monkey butt. The robber kitten's
glaring eye. Keeping cats for the public good
catlings, eyes filled with green fire.
brindled things. a bad and ragged cat
a half-fed cat with fleas.

cats got no worry about losing time. There's
always plenty of the shiny stuff around.
all off along the shadows by the moonlit fence
all just a whisker twitch & a tail flip away
cold & calm as a glacier's heart.
clouds of gradual rain.

It's hard to believe that my little cat dreams of
killing while she sleeps & purrs.
I look into her eyes & see fiddle strings.
a land of no dogs & lazy mice.
walking softly always minced with a
catty kind of insolence. dreaming magnificence
high-stepping cats in wet grass: fancy dancers.

wherry this dream across the river
while away the fisherman's true lies:
Got bit by a poor man's dog gone rabid
kin to yellow fever & allied to smallpox on his mother's side
languid green segmented eyes
finally found the everlasting cat of the night.

where wonder goes

choked by realism the graveyard lives near the road.
the simplicity of little lovely things, the green skirts
of willow, the airy flyway beneath the bridge, the one
lung pop of the African Queen on the inner harbor running
on faith & mist. The unity & darkness of the heron on this
lonely night opens my red heart to the ebb & tide
of vivid life. Swallows, before dawn, winging their
breakfast from the air before the sun. the wind from
god knows where. out on the flats disappointment rests
at the edge of low tide. out of the last unclouded
day you cry to me in the morning. your voice like
the small heart of a bird. unmeant sorrow in a weary
land. softly half awake no power moves you any more.
my reflection gone from your eyes still knee deep in June.
vision caught midstride in the city, a suspended dream
the yielding heart which breaks would sing & should.
a dream of common things & something which gleams.
love remains — no sacrifice. no paralyzing fear—
no shame. you quench a thirst which dries my bones.
the mystery of twilight. the softening of each hard line.
mixing hard complaints with prayer
no cause to hurry home — no path to get there
the incoming lapping up our dreams.

"Harry the herd 'til a weak one drops."
Virgil

high crime; high time; high hopes
He fell for a high misdemeanor.

spider rustling the grass so loudly
she thought it must have been a mouse.

shoals of phosphorescent herring circling the island
in their vasty eloquent numbers.

the tip of winter will not negotiate, has never come
to terms. Flag shuddering on the moon amidst the
debris & golf balls. shreds of the only real true map
pasted to his forehead Gorbachev escapes the coup &
leans towards many independent revolutions.
watching the owls twist among the plains of
alleged reforestation. Blame the owls for closing
your children's school. Blame the owls for not refinancing
your neighbor's swimming pool, the new school gym.

all these accidental, incidental extra deaths
tangled in the mist nets/longlines/walls of the drift nets
cycled finally down the deepy corridors in slow decay
ghost nets in a senseless jungle of death
Muscatel as a second language, a tumble of
thick breath & sweet words. Beyond the power of bus
therapy, like the sea, he can't stop returning.
. . . will not be dandled again. . . .

wiring the earth to the sky, & humans to town by cable tv.
The timber towns dwindle back to tall grass, blackberries,
& second growth alder or ash. satellite dishes &
crickets ringing in the evenings.
Even the frogs are losing their way.
not quite well enough off to stand beauty.
Forced to live in Catfish Town; even the salmon fading
with the trees. Great teepee burners only stone circles of rust.
too many years at the edge of town quiet & alone
cut too many until we cut the last cold stone
stump of fantasy. The politicians show up maybe
once each election year. the cottonwood monotony
of summer leaves us by the river.

In the shadows where the trilliums curl their petals
this is not a tame, sweet land. here the wind has teeth.
Spiders, the ancient scientists, know geometry because
of their bellies. They cannot separate the thought
or reality of god from flowers. holy as the ocean waves
or a strange falling metal angel, flying steel-ribbed angel.
below, the ferns of crystal cluster the line of fence, frosted.
nasturtium's leaves predict the rain by making way for it.
"fervid bees," the clouds behind the world,
something here burns like emeralds & sin
night & starlight in the fishes' breath.

"I was sick as a trout"
May Sarton

the deer breathing over my blackberries
didn't see the moon this morning must be new.
spent the evening with heron & kingfisher, watched
the blackberries bleed. having done what my
karma demands . . . .

wasps nibbling & gnawing at last year's dead foxglove
stalks, making this year's paper. little wasp
drummer filling the garden with this megaphoned
sound. a garden full of weeds; two gardens
full of weeds, dry branches, leaves.
   sansouciance: skinny gods of dirt.
sparking the clouds fall down. fern leaves
& clouds; full moon, poor fishing, lots of words
warming themselves by the fire. old friends
silent sipping beer. saying it all again.

the bloated rich, the hungry angry poor.
in this age there are many more of both of them
maintaining their boyish figures: one through
diet & denial. the other through necessity.
"forgotten, jailed, or killed" by courtesies & evasions.

this is not a pain free life: neither were we promised.

rain slipping from the sky like lingerie
moon so pale thin & waning I went home alone
to a dream of sake, an empty glass &
my own medicine to take, reading the
inside of my eyelids. waiting until there is
nothing else, but the winter's obsidian flakes of
loneliness. We understand these things; we don't have to go.

water draws the shadows down among the thin
darkness of plants. When it is night, it is dark.
the ferns remain stubborn in their greyness
without shame; without honor; the dark world feeds many.

grinning like a clam with a secret beneath
its foot. Too early in the fall for the owls to hoot.
herons pace the low tide of morning
Dawn returns excited to ride the bus to school.
What kind of birds are chooks whose feathers overlap?
salmon skin raincoats sheltering the seeds of longing.
insects among the stars? spiders weaving the milky way.
the images of fir & forest, specific Oregon rivers &
times left unfinished – so we are forced to spend the night.
it can't be saved.

"The words in a line of poetry are small, hunted intensely lascivious wild animals, huddling together in a dark hole, and interbreeding like mad."

James Agee

praise the common good living of good people
beneath the sky. dream maidenhood & wolfing.
the toothless worms of summer gnaw on towards fall
in a shadow cast by starlight summer turns.

slow nails in the lost wind; truth in the shadows
upward mobility among the murdering class.
a dusk of blue steel settled on the low tide beach
chained to the earth by swelling seeds & new summer.
our eyes turn still as slack tidewater in full fog.

> darkness among the leaves loiters
> bent with the weight of dew
> amid the crippled smoke of morning
> electricity blooming light in its bulbs.

the big frog sound of summer evenings in the fall of forest
tracking the retreat of the amphibians, guarded by
recreational vehicles and the NRA.
A mirror of the world I'm in and talking that way
the dawn does not slumber, will not sleep.
"I must write on; it don't have to be read."
"True lust will triumph over indigestion."

she turned fish-belly white. numbed by doubt.
the petals of the poppies fade though
the garden burns with their desire.
> "The man who took his work for wife
>   Dies in high grief of childish tears."

Living in a world of unsteady promise
Sometimes I try to be clever
Sometimes I have something to say
Sometimes it comes out as doggerel
& sometimes it just can't be that way.

"dancing in the rags of an old remorse."
William Everson

trout fin, carp fin in water cuts its lines.
Physicians applauding the cash register.
fungus spreading its silent wings, an avenging
angel taking the path of least nutrition.

the phlegm coughed up from his heart
when the sad moon lays in the calm stranded bay.
trailing our hands in the wake. marking the sunsets
the new dawns on the glint of water's surface.
the heron frozen statue, grey blue, at the creek's
mouth as the tide is taken & the stone of sun
rolls on. The warm must of Chinook wind,
the whoop whoop whit of owls. some smoke; some ash.

it's all cricket food now, & they'll eat most
anything. all the tawny wine of summer &
the rough hands of the moon drawing on the water.
the smile that would not wait still beckons.
in this forward leaning year my own blackberries
too, are rioting at the fence lines. the sun & they
holding together with water my land against death
hostage. fog fills the creek bed.
drenches the brush in this dew. & the rain comes down
later that day like a wave of heavy sleep in full
strong wind. justice comes looking backwards for the wind.
compliance becomes the rule; the rest certainly is dead.
soon there will be frost.

"The bones are lovely, dark and deep. . . "
Theodore Roethke

the musty smell of cradles, blankets,
soft warm air; my father's skin, I notice
growing pale as paper. If the head of a match
breaks off do the fishes scatter like lost silver change?
My woman has fish ways, sways in her watery walk.
moving the morning, shivering dew from day lilies.
The wind sharpens the stones.

with the silverfish & cockroaches
running in & out & in. & the herons cruise high
above the creek mouth, knowing well the calcium
truth of dogs & their entertainment, their hunger.
Here on the island you must walk softly or you'll
wake the clams into midget geyser spitting frenzy
though, this summer the water is low, we become the light.

Cherish, if you must, the mold's children.
jerking secrets from the fish's lips
two individuals in love prove
against themselves that there is no obscurity.
"All who remember, doubt."
I know myself to be rich as a cat.
her several parts are still quivering my memory.
It seems, of course, the weather's weeping
the trees, too, bending under the weight of leaves in wind.

The salmon are tired when they reach the Snake
& the river cold and scented more strongly of home.
"Even carp die in this river,"
living in the morgue of obligation beneath this
shield of summer rain. The rim of the canyons
ringing with the lightning flash, the going into sky.

The tide changes bruising back into smelt among
the soft broken waves, the graveled beach, at Stinson
Point – parked at the end of the Burton Peninsula.
This silver grey energy brought to bear in the boiling
pseudosurf. soft as the breathing of sleeping snails.

Man has always had his wings clipped; no wings, period.
assessing the high astrology of music
at the fond cafe hands are held & most every meal
is vegetarian. beyond the thistles & tofu delight
locked in symbiotic combat (like a small yellow bird)
having decided not to cry.

"Life is cruel; that's the whole point."
George C. Scott
in The Savage is Loose

snake shoulders; snake hips. chicken lips
frog hair; hen's teeth, fish legs; robot breasts; mule milk
landing the big one; skillfully hooked and played.
she loves me like the space between the stars
huddled before the cruel dawn besides a cooling
hearth of stone thin whips of dying fire.

hanging dark clouds about the edge of sky
seeking the way of night. reaping the sorrow of the
wicked windy streets, drunk on anger & pain
madness & desolation. pestilence & cripples,
the hand of judgment cruising by in a black & white.

through Babylon & sins worse wrought
I note these sins for which they weren't caught.
an heritage of sins self-taught.
the cold embrace of Lot's wife's judgment may be ours.
the dead stand before us each morning, in
confidence, with the curling dawn.
that shimmering thing which I see within what is their eyes.

"struck in the head with a sunflower."
George Lessig

the day & night offer choices. The great heron croaks
in the pterodactyl night. here in my bed with the comforting
sound of rain. love does not rule the night; the freedom
to keep it, risk letting go the stone. There is no small certainty
Seek sunshine and embrace the darkness. Find the river
in the fish, aching all over & still singing oneness of the world
& its brimmed choices. a fist unfolding stone solid & fiercely
gentle. still swearing like a crow at the sunshine.
fifteen self-possessed years making tracks to the landing
in the rain. Centered on her own blond future.
balanced in her fear & uncertainty, but falling like rain.

sighted the first osprey here on the creek
yesterday. perched atop a leaning, falling cedar snag.

a lady reclining declines his inclination by
indication of her eyes. they are empty as rites.
a fast blue deep water hardness in her eyes.
Old men wish the wine were theirs; young men drink it;
at my age they store it away. gone jogging or to the bank.
wrath & righteousness swell the unpaid debt.
don't take it personal & you, you, don't let her see
you cry. resist the sea of trouble & oppose the
notions of the force, gravity, time, instinct, all graceless
but really how they are. winding & weaving through
this labyrinth of life constantly searching for that lost key.

121

"A few good things are left on earth"
                                        Ed Dorn

rain becomes a human image, ruins shadows
on a wind ragged, tide's out, crow ravaged morning
Leaves glimmer in the ragged shadow of the wind.
some stars never touch the sea — this is reassuring.

dragging myself slowly from this mound of night.
The Flamenco guitar changes this night forever.
the sky stitched together with this guitar of moon
She would hold me like a chain of wind,
swallows snatch the morning from the air in gentle arcs
climbing the apple tree to untangle the moon.

there is stolid virtue in wet leaves, in mown grass.
while the sun steams the sorrow of the morning
& my little cat sleeps.   "

a crack opens in the sky. stars tumble out
jumping through the window of the morning
eyes emptied; fuses blown; lights dimming out.

avoiding the musty dark
                    he suffered an attack of heart
if only we had the salmon's gravity
        that certain knowledge that home is upstream.
riding an island into fog
    a good shadow can cancel anything
trout flipping bait to the sky & rings in the water
a toothy stone of glass cuts my fingers in the garden
as I sift more stones from the earth.
moon drinker swallowing down its pale light
vowels lost in a hoard of letters & other saved sounds
flames trembling at the stake, heretic, but warm.

Life at the Muskrat Hotel

the urine of industry fouling the bay
beneath the blue knife of tomorrow
a fine blue powder misted afternoon.
heaven is a house of cards, an inside straight
we draw to. in the darkness the room empties
pesticides weeping inside our bodies, the bodies
of our pets. our breath sweet smoke as the days
grow more cold. the glorious jiggle of summer
passing — the bottle of wine cheap & empty
lying in the path of broken things. dark as the secrets
of pituitary. language freezing up with arthritis
all exceptions drift. Hole in the Day/Hole in the Sky.

on a street named Pellagra, a suit of fireflies
spending the cantaloupes of desire
walking the rim of Creator Lake/Creator Lake Blue.

she was a long empty dark & he measured his life in
steaming cups of coffee. all the talk's of without.
eating sunshine when it's around. life in the
monopolytic curve. a long empty darkness.
the dust of trees & owls in our veins
one shoulder at a time folding into & out of clothing
racing through this epiphany of rain & fading roses
surgery sex as an adjustment; slicing the air with a frog
hell bent for autumn & the rain, the colors of the leaves.

though we are toys with small beating hearts
the smiling will be upon us. none the less. we know
& these edges etch us tight. It can't be revealed
to other hearts & it must. it will not rest sterile.

my family does not contemplate my disgrace
neither do they remember me as sailing.
I do not trust either the water or the wind
In every circumstance, you return to one.
confined in the arms of circumstance: get back one.
morning gone soft/sky with its light.

we do not even eat the oysters in our fear
stuck always between grandeur & the graveyard
tomorrow drifts down from the mountains
red tail lodged in the air at a stall.
All of us die in the combat zone
                    In the combat zone.
                    of the combat zone.

"The color of truth is grey."
Andre Gide

all that history tangled in the old woman's hair.
Harvest moon September full rising as the sun
sinks down like a dead girl. the wind bends her
down. the wind blows in; the lights go out.
once she touched me & then I lost her.
out into the quiet disdain; the mercury vapor lights
the neon glitter of hard paved streets.
the night is young; it is we who are aging.

leaving the backroads behind. LeToya recounts
those years of family abuse, verbal,
emotional, sexual. she explains &
explains why her body is no longer hers,
no longer Black, no longer looks like that
family. bones scraped; nose thinned &
adjusted; breasts augmented & implanted
skin bleached. For Playboy she lets her
pubic hair be combed, recombed, and poses
for this photo session with twenty
of her favorite snakes. everything airbrushed
lightly, tastefully.

I fold back time & cherish old passion, the warm
smooth stone of your thighs and all of that
light which we bathed in. the pure comfort of
your breasts & the unhurried way we dressed.
How all of this went by so fast
& I am left with hardly any light.

Lost Boys

Postlude

The universe is a vast system of poorly signed freeways.
"Next rest stop one star too far." No way out of town
& the insatiable life on the streets
where there are no public restrooms & a smile robs you
in the silent hours where sadness opens in the
cracks of the sidewalks. even the dreams here will
use you. modest agony, late terrors, the usual delusions.
and tedious revelations. time, having lived us,
doesn't even show disdain. & the tide recedes.

left standing alone at the corner of Stares & Whispers
watching traffic solemn as the stone silent owl
perched atop the County-City Building.
small animals & calm water, these glow with humility
bitter & phosphorescent. The stars claw their way from
the horizon into a sky as long & blank as tomorrow.

Fueled by causeless hate, the streets do not mourn
each night the withered streets bloom; the alleys fill with
this violent potential, this obstinate yet patient anger
which spills out into the suburbs with its outright poverty.
guilty of innocence with nothing left to forgive, no home,
nothing to give but desire, nothing to abandon but need.
The wind unwinds the air, provokes the past, moves into our time.
not even a murmur follows us to the door. It is not our place.

In the far off landscapes, at the base of the mountain, is a logger
once a logger, unemployed, loading his shotgun for one last walk.
Peacefully he leaves his dog at home, faithful, & hopes for
no game. the heart to carry on. & clouds to cover him.
he walks alone through the red flowers he is leaving.
the spindly second growth which he will never fall.
it is a very small parade. his last afternoon battles with the sky.
his life a pile of sawdust & withered leaves. this is his last goodbye.
he's not waiting for anyone. nothing you can say,
the frail shadow only returns home alone
the only thing left this side of time & the shadows of the ancient
forest. The ax and the plow knocking at the dim lit doors.
he has gone dancing. left the ax, the crippling plow.
with the light he has gone dancing, out with the flaming tide.

Summer leads the rivers down from the mountains
having fallen from a tattered sky & frozen to still rest
the consequences answer for the salmon through the treeless
backwoods. the last few fish reprieved for this season.
consumed by the sensuous luxury of summer, of their
own free will the salmon, these few salmon, return.
in their thirst for home they do not sleep. their eyes
won't close. the tyranny of fish asks nothing but a
wet way home. meditating upstream.

she wears nothing but a cape of broken glass—this
suit of lights which glitters on the horns of the bull.
the shadows enter the room. In any language this is murder.
this struggle. inanimate & dead as most of the treaties
for which they owe their lives/the land which they
will never see. the warmth of hands they fear to feel.
the panting night watches from its corner the inevitable.
the fish have no ears, or they would be trophies also
in the fair false light of a morning come too early
each day. It's like blaming the lack of trees upon the
owl — the slow, low lack of water upon the fish.
Each fish carrying its own indelible scars, their
lack of rest, dead of exhaustion & consummation.
heavy shudders in the redds their object dream.
nothing easier than breaking, than forgetting, than failing
entirely to return. trapped by the butterflies of paralysis.

the bull will not break his horns upon the dancing flesh.
instinct does not falter, but pushes onward, upsteam.
The English language is finally infected by justice
each life still & only a few sparks in watery silence.
Both the salmon & the bull may end understanding
it is the language of knives, a language which twists
& then there are the hooks, the nets, & the night.
No bones now intact return to the stream: belief, error,
& faith. The matador is a hunter, a fisherman, & the bull
has slim chance, the arena little shade, the old streams
less water moving sluggish toward desert.
The wind sings the song of sand & the bull paws the dust.
if the fish had lips they would snarl in the muzzle of night.
there are no doors to open; the gates are closed, no ladders
to the next cascade of water high as tears, wearing away.

A butterfly aching settles the end of summer
a sorrow which surprises. frantic as a loom
the swift shuttle lost, the selvage unbinding.
the small trees engulfed by thorn green vines.
shambles/brambles the breath of gliding stars.

It's a cool rain in hell, this day, a dreaming
darkness settles from her thighs. moon full
tomorrow as the bulbs begin their sleep.
the toxic music of the airwaves rush.
fair weather sailer allows for no storms, none.

Winter sky pale as your summer covered skin
deaf pride & coldness yearning warm
for more, for change to ride. the enigma:
my cat wants out; the other wants in
but this will change

The sun each day warms this intolerable world.
the birds wake and realize that they are late for the south.
the sighing of foxes in their dream sleep, fat dream
mice with fat short slow legs. a flicker in the
trees. how long the dead long for one more life.

How wilderness endures the need for more.
a day storm, a night of quiet moments turned to
laughter and into a past. Curt Cocaine throws
his lights out & away with a shotgun; Canada
quivers in cold storage as their young men

Follow him from fear & despair of living. the leaves also
regret the trees they lift to nestle & heat the dark
soil. the ease of insect life, the lack of future
cares burnt out by the need for food and fertility.
ghostly fire backlit in fog, the daylight curls

Uncurls from the creekbed. each of us soon to be
dust or ashes depending on the cost & the coverage
of our insurance. since his death he is among
the best of men. we drop them bodies down
try as we always do to linger. the water breaks

Our hearts turn stone, still turn cold , & turn & turn.
a curse in glory turned & undone, underdone
unfinished, but final. a delicious dance, still.
no ruin here to look back upon, but beds of
flowers blossoming, blooming, & sleeping in each year.

shadows twilit the walls of deckled brick grey
red. lights draw him for the warmth here bright
hope for delight and other's charm. Each day another
want. labeled indigent as a crime & crippled by
the same shadow cast as name. a stranger city
than destiny discovered with glinting windows, none
his own. A view with the wind sighting down his
longing with the chambers empty, the woods emptying,
and the shelters full. learning compassion at this
corner waiting for the light. the sun rises
the day darkens such a deep water port to call.
he lived alone, died dark. pouring his eyes from
shadow to shadow, his heart from the green night train.

Difficulty blooming mid October, planted late
in a dry summer. A thought, a look, a breath,
hesitating to cross the solitary. unconsolable,
yet driven finally to the edge of town, the county line.

my new son coughing from the couch in sleep
my daughter, new also, rests late in blonde haired dreams.
dreams. The wrong move makes you an angel.

he is dragging his eyes across the beauty of women
homeless and alone, each with a long
long story and smoldering eyes telling the dream.

Rust upon the lilacs, mold settling among the roses.
vermilion in the morning – vermilion at noon.
lonely only lonelily most all hands are blind.
the stone moves within his heart & the chill rises
to her lips, finding old things only
making words pass as air.

"when girls pout, make yourself available."
advice from the goddess

watch for starlight through the window.
If art, it was our fact. & that, not alone.
the impulsive flicker of lust, only one small
portion of the vision.
& at the waiting end "Cancer, senility, mania,"
& ragged clouds green the new morning sky.

he limps along and hums a blessing
rhythm for each step. Save us from the
mutation of outmoded biology & each new virus.
save us from the ape-lust of each new day.
things get downright difficult. clouds, slow low
gliding down/up/along/above Judd Creek.

here in the full moon dark on this island of
suffering & enchantment, waiting for the lights
to come on. spent all night preparing for the dawn;
this entire night has gone foreign.

autumn rain fills the morning falling
simple & strange anonymous among the streets
each disaster brings its own generations, tagging
along like bells. sirens. it is night in the city
& some of these faces—these stories—small
but personal histories can hollow the hope
out plumb out of you horizontal: murder,
the holy grail, chastity, & lost fortunes.

Even the taxis won't stop for you here
the pawn shops of despair won't offer you a dime.
even. anonymous among the streets. crossed by
the debris of destiny. one wrong star.

we all lay down. we all lay down & wait. we all lay down
& wait like animals. In this we do not fail, technically
I live in the country. like a freeway, landing strip.
boat dock hoodoo lounge life, full of cheap dreams
& five acre plots of roses, sweet williams, hedges &
what's left of the forest we sold to plant the hedges,
pave the drive.

This is a young men's alley,
where we brag & spit out the sun.

Here it has turned a night wet with moonlight —
mist from the river. The dark is wrong;
most of our heroes have been empty.
It's pretty funny, strange—grey like—.

It's true; I see less & less old men, more boys,
more years to throw at the moon.
when he pulled out the credit card, his can opener,
the police had no choice but to shoot him.
& the orange-eyed cat waits to be outside in this
crisp October pre-morning dark chill.

a weekend in search of the trembling sturgeon,
fishing from 12:30 to three with more bait
than even a squid might be able to handle.
nudging sleep from our eyes testing the truth
of the space blanket, the blue tarp, & the river.

A small stray sneaks well in the morning—
black & white adolescent kitten—mannerly
eats all of the smelt not desiccated from freezing—
leaves everything tidy & quiet, making off with
a fair earned meal. a blackberry wild kitten
on a night with no wind & moon like a hard-boiled egg.

she filled me like wet sand whispered
my name into the darkness. Found four deadly
sins in the parking lot of the Baptist
seminary, beautiful as it was with its old
growth cypress & roses & bricks walling courtyards
above the Sound. a needle, broken whiskey empty
bottles, a condom, and rock & roll on tape.

Nude, but mauled by music; at risk polishing
the stunted glory, "bad breath dreams." Oh, to be
sure, there's frail little to depend on. All of it
can fall away and disappear. the job, the $, the
friends, the social hours. All of it frail & waiting.
poised to fall, fail, & fade into your next dilemma.
the clouds, though, have not contemplated murder.

the famous temple

surely, this is my best side, less sinister than
the right. this blue throbbed vein. this always
crying of the gulls. the rigid diet of divorce.
First ruffle then rest, the winds will come again.
this dusty chill-boned resurrection. Bingo in the sky
or at the Reservation where everybody wins
if you play enough cards. White
Chinook, white buffalo calf woman, now reborn.

though our hearts are not whole
the water bird, pale as morning, stills its wings
at the mouth of the creek. Our lily liver chicken hearts
pale against the sky, so pale, which weeps & weeps
all long morning, serious waiting, blessing of rain.
water past saving living past praise the moon
gone soft in its failure fading. She wakes; she
says she loves me as she touches her hair.
she touches my hair & the night will not leave me.
this is the drowsy future & we will wake again tomorrow.

there is priceless water in glaciers, blue ice to be shipped
to Japan. melting with the rain. swift told in the
falling sky, a house filled with apples.

"Through this ugly duckling world."
Charles Bukowski

love at times takes courage as the blood fills the room
five o'clock in the morning rain. nipple dizzy &
pussy simple as he is, I am. The grave remains real.
each of us leaning against death and the new morning
sky in a rain which makes us remember. remember
that men behind desks are skin to the lord
& his best beloved because they handle his insurance
policies & the complaints & the potential floods
from the heavy rains. remember that little caged monkeys
have the chance of a hummingbird. this day, this rain,
it will not happen again. though we empty all the iron
beds seeking fishermen. ranting my/his
cancer to the sky: someone else's death doesn't
touch too deeply when hunger gnaws the
place you need to sleep & you too are cold.

The red rose burning of this another war, love.
This solvent sorrow which melts most everything
in the rain – beaten down the little pig
lane toward the knife, that last cigarette.
The good days are few though days aplenty.

bums & madmen fill the streets to the curb.
they pull them down by their tattered wings
each one to the display, filling quickly now.
retaking Hollywood; it's a noble dream filled
with long legs, high cheek bones, fashion & a
hint of tender smoke from elegant lungs &
expensive cigarettes. Today we put the sky
into its place, though it kept falling & puddling
around the front steps. if you're not careful
they will come and take you away.

Famous enough to bum cigarettes most anywhere,
what they always deserve is one more try

Honest she took my shape & would not leave, could not
return though she coerced the bones & they broke.
& her knuckles bled until she was blonde & taller
with a mouth as red as Christmas. eyes like napalm
burning in the rain. shredded papers filled with mothers
killing/drowning their children, insanity claims
kidnapping, theft, and a sympathetic audience.

the television demands a swarm of stars & revenge.
it will never be a fair trial because she is accused.
and the winter sun bright shines & warms the moon
& my face, not a dosstalker, but a full disk.
dancing in microchip hell—wounded in difficult beauty.
vast & empty. naked, vast, & empty. vast beauty
elegant, nostalgic, remote. & it echoes
resounds & wanders down the primrose path
at the base of the steep-walled canyon.

Phenobarbital & the lice which trace our human history
tripping through the wide-eyed saga of manifest destiny.
eliminating even the shadows which declare such
a past. though the blood stains do not wash. will not.
& the sad promises remain. broken salvation
& someone else's heart to depend on.
& a desperate forgetting.

still searching for the lost boys

crisp clear, full moon
& freezing here in never
never land. something
about the second star
& steering into morning.
Downtown the heroes
of the street wake,
shiver, and pass the last
bottle among them.
this is the blood and
their flesh is cold.
their faith fading with
the darkness thumping
pockets for that last
cigarette. the mission
will open. the coffee
is steaming somewhere
in this lost down town.

the surgical precision
of badges is cruising
the streets. the food is
a ministry. The Last Chance
is a ministry & the coffee
offers some faint hope.
soon the sun will
hit the water: the sun
will tear through
its piece of sky.
sleep is a temple &
death is a sweet rest
hunger is a dream &
food a gone hallucination.
the last of the leaves
will be forced from
the trees. the dusted frost
of moonlight falls
& dusts the killing
streets. The morning starts
its engines & the freeways
fill with commerce.

Despair droops his
shoulders, walks with
Sadness with a vision
of Warmth in their
numbed hands. Bearing
another day like
a memory of summer,
wearing their anonymous
armor. dark clothing
shapeless & second-hand. So
intent to survive that
nostalgia comes to them
only as nightmare—
a promise of broken fretful
sleep. hometown & a family
for the holidays. Blank
pages falling from
the calendars like
the passage of time
in old movies. We thought that
the Pope canceled purgatory.
It is a struggle
of shadows washing
down the street with
their hope in their
hands, faint mad light
in their eyes. knowing
that shadows do not
make light. "looking
into the sad dolphin's eyes."

Not drugs or drinks
enough to frost his mind.
plumbing the deep
inexhaustible well of doubt
etched into those
brown clouded eyes.
got about half a gram
of desire left & nothing
to turn. the savings &
loan in hell is also
failing. falling toward the
bottom, hoping for the dead
cat bounce. while doubt
clouds the sky   The days
are dreams—the nights are
real with no hope
for dreams. immortality
rests on a shelf down
at the liquor store
having its price changed.
getting fortified against
Remorse. sharing a drink
of Sadness with Despair
with Denial. speaking again
& again. Tearing the
pages from telephone books
to use & leave in
the fields of vacant lots
& abandoned buildings. to
wipe the shame in shadows.

choosing the numb needle
of love & the money it
will bring though
more numb each automobile,
each twenty dollars.
each John Andrew Jackson.
this is not talking to
god. hostile suspicious
sex, something shooting &
shifting up the spine.
getting old & getting sad
at the same time. chilled
more than to the bone.
love as a contrary act.

most of us are gifts
from the dead. & hell
is not an abstract
disease. gliding like
phantoms through the mist
of the brutal sleepless
streets dropping the eyes
from sidelong glances.
selling flesh & trying
to save the bones in
a whisper. silent but
not invisible. dying
younger than hope can
realize. dementia is
not crazy on these
streets. where the weather
is dying we are not
seeking solitude.

wishing someday to fall
in love. lost to
forever. from drugstore
to drugstore with no
prescriptions to fill.
wearing each wounded
day like a crisis.
dreaming for the body
of summer on streets
where each activity is
dangerous. Discovery Bay
of grief seized by greedy
violent dreams stumbling
stupor to stupor
as a whisper which
the streets support.
each hallucination drowns
a reality smoke to ash.
the sorrow of waves
caught in the tide.
each night sleeping
undead among the other
dead. a violent present
& the future the same.
incarcerated in order
to continue, palms out,
pockets empty & the
bondsman laughs. treacherous
night comes creeping
from the east where
it will bleed in the
morning, tragic & pure.
sex as barter or a gift.
something illicit,
charged with simply being
alive. with a thirst
for that fiery dew
of passion & amnesia.

hypothermia has the
distant texture of stars
somehow it looks so
easy. & the economy
is strong, recovering,
& the streets fill with
the ballast of unemployment
projections. these are
not cargo. & the
successful drive by in a
cold sweat—dropping
them one by one with
their eyes. one void
dreaming into another.
rock mother, lost mother
your children are here.

Sonny Bono goes to Congress.
These are those times
In their sleep they
curl around their hurt,
tight as a dream.
smuggling each dream
with its tinsel
from shelter to shelter,
not an emergency until
there is no way to
rise from the street.
a man down call
and rescue one sirens
what's left into the
flashing red lights.
abandoned buildings.
abandoned bodies,
one good pair of shoes
& an intangible life
lost in statistics & averages.

crying like a scar in
the sunshine. dreaming the
other reality, sleep &
forgetting. too cold for
dew drops. starting to
sweat & itch. the
great need swelling. the
shadow becomes violent,
agitated. half frozen
in the backseat of
an abandoned plymouth doing
small sex for drugs and
a little more time,
no witnesses.

downtown business staffed
by mannequins in
three-piece suits,
programmed for the day.
high finance ringing
up totals in their eyes.
embracing the tides
as dependable & real
the arpeggio of moon
above the mountain
above the peninsula
across the harbor far from
the island. but still
beneath the sun. a hazy
distance through the mist
& clouds. still at the
horizon. remembering each
pigeon as a soul lost
on the streets, but
flocking together. while
the steam rises from
the creekbed remembering
that last motel. aching
for the first cigarette of
morning as the streets
turn to cold aching
flame also.

waking each day as
a substitute for prayer.
& each syllable is naked
& through these months
each morning will be
colder. A square yard
& a half of skin
walking/trudging through
the sunlight. frosted
concrete hard and cold
against thin soles.
sniffing glue for
its warmth. blustering
for the power. begging
because it works. too
proud to dive into
the dumpsters of certain
future. stealing hair from
the barber shop & dreaming
of August, much farther
than months away.

it is not language
which does this,
and the thrill of
revolution leaves on
the first bus out
of town. clinging to
the shadows of waiting
because something else
is bound to happen,
and it does.
it always does. if
we can remember.

This Brown Paper Bag

"We walk till we get to another time.
and then we get a vehicle."
100% Weird TV

the shadows hold here among the stones
and the stones move the sky slowly
geology might be the study of this man
near petrification but holding to the pulse
and planting flowers in November.

drums are not enough for a river which
longs for the sea. generic food with
commodity labels. pockets empty of everything
but loss, moon fading like another broken
promise. promise them the earth, give
them the moon if they can carry it away.
take it all out to the burning barrel, only a
pile of grey ash. wading through forgiveness
every morning, jumping through the rings which
fade on the water. no need left to find a
way to die. it's cruel on the streets, but the staid
homes are more violent, more dangerous, pretend
that they're full of love. they are warmer but
it costs, big time. it costs. & the hunger inside
is different, more empty. coughing up yesterday
and spitting it out the window. most of the time
there are no witnesses. still got the promise of
bingo & tax-free cigarettes, less land, less fish,
less & less of ourselves—burning the paper
bus schedules, ferry schedules, biding our time.
waiting to ride home with the salmon—hitchhiking
over the dams. got to get to the dance.

night crawled up the front steps, a pure white cat
peering in the windows as night's gone too far & the
bay begins to silver. avoiding the trap in that net
of red. seizing the darkness in our pockets,
winking an eye & screwing up the courage to ask
for small change, again. staggering from the grey
sleep unsteady yet bold enough, hungry enough to try.
desiring what is not here. what is not here? though
the sun feels good. my blackberry sprawled
orchard calls me for some relief. the line is busy.

anger opens like a white moon morning glory in
the sun. best not to ask, to meet the eyes, best
to get where you're going, no questions asked.
door slams; wet tire hisses stop light: walk.
walk. walk. when the uniforms
arrive like insects alarmed & armed
death or love; killing or sex: both treason & sadness
strung on electric guitar tight blues licks.

hold everything at a distance
so that it may become real & you are shaking
with mileage & time. he speaks of Hemingway
& the bullfights, playing it close to the horn.
each move with its grace & its rules & its music.
& the scientists do get to Mars & the telephone
is a demand not a plea left. messages to be kept
" just something that grows or does not
    grow lives a while and dies a long time."
gonna be eaten by the cat. morning or no.

gone dizzy with hunger or love. & the mind gone
empty. A kingfisher waiting for the tide to change.
wounded by the morning or a stray one of cupid's darts,
I wander downtown wearing my teeth all day
comparing wallpaper to weight lifting women
still alive and wondering why. & that kingfisher
perched on the piling turns his head & looks at me
as the bus flows by & the tide takes me home.

from web to web asking for spiders swinging
between heaven & hell wondering why it was that god
kicked the light bringer out on his pointed ears.
sorrow says that she feels lonely & old today. I agree.
& she flashes the lightning of her body. one of my
stars winks out. & the lights on the street show
shadows, lonely loveless people shadows.

life is sad & dangerous, everything eats & everything
dies. don't look in that bowl in the back of the
refrigerator. there's something in there that's alive.
dancing in the honkytonk phone booth.
loneliness moves slowly; its habit & its pain
light the front yard. she waters her plants & cries
looks out the window and cries. life is a game

"these mad dogs of glory" & their lost toys
Charles Bukowski

he never missed a day of work & he died standing up.
impossibly human, possibly animal.
trees which are less than that also lose their leaves.
it was thin & hungry, sometimes desperate, but wonderful
suffering arid dreams.

defeated by a dream which doesn't come true
& each day there is a little less to kill, less diversity
more sheep in the meadow, more cows in the corn.
imagining the agony of the elephant, caged parrots, midgets
tossing pebbles into the rings of their nightmares.

Anna's hummingbird is the only one that winters here
on the Sound. how does it live?
hitmen, ballet dancers, and fishermen, they get by.
and they change their profession: except the fishermen.
being sane doesn't mean that you'll feel better about it.

"I think that I still have a bottle of poet left."
Charles Bukowski

It may be a heart of brass, but the blood is still moving
who wants to sleep with a woman of flame?
wake up with that burning sensation, still perfectly
empty. power & selfish disregard versus sadness
so profound that breathing is difficult & tears won't come.

The Serbs hold 400 blue helmeted peacekeepers as
hostages against strikes from the air. Tutsies
knocking off Hutues. It's sad out there, & I just
ordered hundreds of flowers to plant & have a closet
full of nice shoes. cheap, but nice & warm.

Living with others, there's the pain. Living without
others, there's the pain. There's the pain, that's the
living. Face the morning sun & remember Lorca's
"agony, always agony . . . " And we're still crawling
those same starving streets, ankle deep in our
failing charity. if good words light the night
then burn these pages & pass the bottle.
hand me the bait & we'll cast out again.

the social services

we reviewed all of our files because the feds
wanted to talk to a couple of clients who
were doing well. moving from homeless to
employed and a state of homefulness. two stood
out & we asked them if they'd mind talking
to the on-site reviewers.

it went quite well—the money came down
the chute for one more year. we had our jobs.
a week later the most articulate young man
found his girlfriend in the restroom of his employer
making pleasure for another man. plates went
everywhere. spaghetti stained the walls
& he carved the other man up with a steak knife
from one of the tables. one to the hospital, her with
one black eye—the marriage gone from her future.

the other one still owes me the twenty bucks
I lent him to tide him through to his
first check. moved on to community college.
we closed his file too.

searching for "so called genius darlings who are not."

the music is sick & thin, the freeway air exhausted
burning the truck of dinosaurs. smoking the ozone
& the burning question: "how do you work an eight hour
day when you suspect that the moon is not there?"

dull eyes forming up in every damn line in town.
the checkout line, the bank line, the money machine,
the soup kitchen line, the line waiting for beds
at the Last Chance, the welfare, foodstamp, WIC,
& bathroom waiting lines. All dull eyes.
kind of like movie popcorn has a life & meaning
all its own. god created life as a deliberate waste.
Rude & dumb until critical mass
when the mob, the pack, the school,
the flock gets a mind of its own.

he says there's music shaking it in the shadows
of hell. come on, let's go hang some time in the air
with this guy. It's the absence of hope which
so shrouds the streets which we navigate so dark,
so cold, so long & lonely. It's the hope which isn't
there which tucks in our fright. all of those promises.

They know me by my outfit. they know. The grey morning
slowly opening the day like a flower. the buds
weeping for yesterday's sweet afternoon. lights out.
sweet ladies of death twisting the ends of a new smoke.
somehow, drunks are never forgiven;
it's too easy to lay the sweet guilt down.

"The sun like a yellow glove"
Charles Bukowski

Faces joke to us from the street corners
imitating the pretenders & dancing on thin eyes.
the night & the darkness of the city leave a taste in your
mouth. Each city tastes differently: a personality
of the palate. dim souls glittering from the shadows
the long slow careful alleys. spilling a drink:
bad form. breaking the glass: bad style. ordering up
a full meal platter of those deep-fried blues.

the word is useless & writing is an indecent profession.
moon soars like a rising falcon & there is rest
in this chill snowy night. liquor & liabilities.
need stacked upon need shivering. while the Sound
breaks & breaks & is still the sea
the inside of a yellow glove.

The engine of night is a diesel, stubborn & hard to start
& for the first few minutes it sounds as though she's
gonna throw some rods – or just that the tappets
or the lifters are worn. the night is slapped
silly by television. simply an average blue light terror.
we all share the darkness. not playing our favorite
songs because we will remember the light, how we wore
our hair, spoke, endured. turning the corner into love.
a grace in going. death's awareness closer than the page.
into arguments that don't end as fistfights
but as broken caps & oozies & hell torn children.

oh brother, being with cats is not alone or without effort.
or being cut while shaving. in this dinosaur dream machine
some of us wake up in the raggedy darkness.
still not cut of the same cloth
dragging the moon home because it followed him.
how smallness can break your heart
here on the streets we got a thousand midnight alleys.
But even the worst night's jackals
cannot claim you twice.

I wake with glass silvered in my hair
allowing the houseplant to live was one choice
& allowing the tilt of swallows their choices in air
was another. this life against our will.
throstling, the finny glint in the blue heron's eyes.

fish bones like keys in her pockets
waiting in her dream of being taken care of,
weak & powerless in love which she perceives through
lost love, none found. some bitter anger insane in
her voice, all gone accusation & complaint
the cold violence of hot bodies calculated. & so thin
only our enemies can make us heroes.

she carries sadness on her wrist like a small ticking.
in a little clock we build a giant machine.
we call it a watch until we are forced to.
the decadence & late nights turned to tea
in the quiet morning. the past curling like steam
a life mistaken in belief.

breath like a mist of folded wings
along the creek. calmness is a shaded corner
among the rocks. & the birds will stay as long
as we remain/invisible. in a dawn like this
the deer are drinking the moon luring the sun to rise
earlier & spark the grass to feed their quickened
future. to lend their heartbeats to the leaves.
pondering the code of dreams
a cipher of light in those folded wings.

a field, a fence, & darkness

oh, it's still a fat fish moon & lovely breathing air
somewhere between coffee and the moon
a caffeine dream, belly full of lightning
like rain on a dog's back
pendulum pudendum pudenda
alone in the mouth of the woods
the fir snags are fog-hung steeples.
pileated hopping from island to island windless.

he cloyed his way from the garden to the outhouse
watching woodpeckers work, showering
the forest floor. like an afternoon
& an old measured argument like pitch
in that green fir log. each morning the crows
curse hunger. Orange-bellied pine squirrel
suffering the diving spark of unfettered desire.
the trees put on their leaves drinking in the
Ides of March. leaflets flooding the air with
their old want as real as the wheelbarrow
or those white chickens.

"Each star a wave of flight"
Don Wilsun

ten finger sudden on ivory, walking out
the dance, using a glass hammer the
gulls restate their plaintive request through
the motionless morning. glass heron fragile
flight glide mirror shadow fishing for ripples
clinging to the skirts of death. out dancing with
the wolves at the door. & night dents the days with
sleep.

fish blue and shining like a nickel
& the rain itself falls from the pages like stray
letters. myrtlewood groves along the tired river

memory of fever & a blue moon &
      "How are things strutting
        down on Catfish row?"
night fills with the chill splash of the tide
wave on wave, wake or none. the night comes
only half as often as the tides. rain blown
& the red tails court & spark
& not a gull was screaming.
each rain swells the driveway & the cormorants
dry their oiled wings, short of April, short of spring
speaking the sea, expecting time. & late. again.
breathing air.

she arrives like a bad attitude; earthquake means
money; it's the construction business – let Momma
Nature go. blood dirt stone. let her shake & dance
the days are quickening. loving the poor & falling
from grace. waking in a wet wine world in
a wrinkled suit, bad socks, and the same underwear.
hitchhiking into the dawn, & whipping the
mules of god into a hellish froth, waking
the silent angel of dawn, breaking the curve
of morning bursting with a fast tide & a gull's cry.
stars winking out with bird songs of morning.
each soul wreathed in lace.

These pastel women— even when the pen won't write.
for Don Blanding

gadget driven: the insistent frenzy
of Babylon. clamorous & isolated
the dawn side of oh-dark-thirty.
it's beyond words, but I'll tell you
                    about it anyway.

a smell here to hold a tumbleweed heart.
something louder which is just nothing acting
like something. they've raised the rent in Babylon
after the war & everything beneath the loud & braying
stars. a thief who waits for god to turn. light
trying to, terrified, sleep among stars.
tame has room for moments, many,
as the flock lands the sky is mended.
starlings are not a native bird
stretching for words to describe the dawn.

the present curls into a past
the question begs until it's asked
which is this rain-dark lullaby
which brings the buds & strikes to the roots.

"Except pornography is the cure for war . . ."
Robert Kelly

"He had never been the same since
he had opened up that fortune cookie:
'your life will be filled with mackerels.' "

sad weeping fir branches gnawing at the dawn.
morphine's cold lost dream avenues
where every pool mirrors the stars' own
grey-clouded sky, with only a lonely will.
photosynthesis is a cave of light for sugar
stepping through the sweet gravity of her hips.
spending the years learning the morning, the tides,
the chasing moon, a drop of her treasured on my fingers.

there is no mercy in the moon, unflagging change.
the woman, bow – man, the arrow – together
through distance (the arc of) cities are visions
breaking an egg for belief, cities are visions
the morning with no sky, but only sea grey above
& reckoning that you can trust both fear and lust.

she has the firm love of law. my hand asleep beneath
her: "the smell of grass is sweet
                                so death mows the lawn."
she landed just this side of the full moon.

Gondwana mama!

Spent the whole day shaking the can't hardlies
ended up with a good case of catfish fever.
all the hope we need is to find the shadow.
we sell our shadows dearly. knowing nothing.
I write her name among the trees & the trees
whisper limb to limb. fish scales & dreams
of the masks of fish & of doubting the dreams.
each mask calls a name. each event is more
serious than we thought. my wife struggles in her
sleep, yet gives me each new morning.

only three thousand stars visible in the sky
yet, the salmon see the source.
we track the beach & the tide abolishes.
every eye sees a different flower, a different sunset,
a wet grey slug of a sky beneath which
loneliness cries for itself, a great personal
emptiness & such holy science. she spends her
mornings studying the acoustics of light.
the pure space left by ringing darkness . . .
my wife, her life, these children an influence
& some clouded desire beneath an ocean of moon
in the wash & rush of spring.

unattainable (elegiac melancholy)

with every mutt on the cul de sac
it runs among us denying colors.
"You know, that's a white baby."

this morning, back when we were young
        & the light crisp sure
by the light of channel five.

each storm reminds me that there must be
dragons & these canyons echo yes . . .
heavy & specific it turns on black wings.
      this sure long burning love.

when the last old tree falls, they will go too
like a pale horse grazing—the morning fills itself
she feasts on solitude and plants seeds
tends the weeds, more loneliness than
imagination can raise. here the water glows
& the fish slide sideways up the stream
her breasts, her eyes — her dark new hair.
pummeled with desire & this abstinence
the near me, but no. eyes like the sanguine sea,
(once she dreamed with me)
she sings like a far dark star.
she makes my breath slide sideways as I balk,
shy as the morning's gone mist. no half truth to tell
like panties growling in teeth. some sweet machine
I should blush because you know a fierce restraint
such a sweet thorn, your love & wings, graceful wings
three bodies one mind like a garden tending
several ideas. but no curtain of flame.
& we can't wash the clouds.   most luminous angel
of the morning. maybe a tomorrow & hot coffee.

"Feed me to my prime"
Nathaniel Tarn

It is a prolapsed dream
the donors do forget what they gave
whiling the day getting home
more naked than nude
betting on progress is sure (assures) destruction
evil is tired, devours our energy,
changing is changing is tired and changes
(like coincidence) change,
leaves fall as footsteps bridging tree to earth—
to sky deeply married
hesitation touches our hands.

a night in which the light is never burning.
the stars (stares) are not captured
the night not yet begun.

dream time is a small corner.
the leaves (make the noises) of curtains closed
the photographs dream. in their rest
they fix the light. this certain knowledge
these tress hiding with no hands,
folding their leaves into waiting.

(a sparrow is safe among eagles)
in the music we listen to our sleep
to our mother's rhythms.
the wind has wound around her like a color.
silence travels among us with the voice of a swimmer.
rain supporting generations of birds.

some dreams have corners — don't go there.
the dark gathers & the wind rustles the stars
          a clatter of stars & moon
issuing governments & bureaucracies like
          an aging revolution
spinning salamander's wool, fresh from the fire
with your feet in dreams, death comes nearer.
understanding the past enhances your future.
Youth & wine do not remain upon the earth
& paper passes away. shards/shattered
language. youth passes like a dying
star. the light lingers. remains.

the river shimmers & our eyes light.
the sixties in our blood & our family
our friends vietnamed away. broken glass.
each new day as fragile as tomorrow

though the morning light is steady
the fish dimple the water—it is death's hungry
fever. throwing seeds at the moon
the sea of tranquility, no glory to be found.

stars & time, so long for the light to arrive
that each star is not there then.
nature makes us targets, helps us to hide
ridiculous as lizards with grey aprons.

the knife is a flower & each night, he writes,
pierces the stars. death looks over our shoulder
its sweet music trusting us to tell the truth.
so sweet that even the air bruises our hearts.

white linen is a grief which carries the whole
nine yards—all of it waving in the wind.
the bus change sobbing in my pockets
each smile is a game though the teeth are
real enough, & there is a promise of flowers.

she is so fine that her breasts murmur at mass.
let the crickets take our voice & let me wear
the silence as a ring. let me drink the water.
artificial wings & broken flowers, a seam of shadow.

it is a rumor that even the statue desires your breasts.
the waves have polished this need, each single
fish is a far need all of us are waiting for
that one arrival. no fear.   only life dancing.

& I am most proud that you came along with me.
though we remain as mad as the seasons
leaves falling from our hair. though we dream
& the pelvis has its own pumping heart.
we've got to get to somewhere's dance.

"Throwing the china"

here beside this knot of waters drowning worms,
roads going everywhere from here
the sounds of bumblebees in rhododendrons
each center another margin
rich in place, placement, & the waiting for each other.
Birds all day birds & children & the surfsound
of traffic over rooftops

salmon hearts thrashing the river
some lands needing discovery,
some praying to be overlooked
hunkered like flowers in the frozen ground.

having died laughing death did not sting.
the forest is a vast library. a vast poverty to
come in their falling. meeting the man who is
never there & always waits shrinking the edge of the
forest, what's left each time. the birds are our
sleep. their wings flutter – our eyelids like wings.
kindling the eyes of the dead. our breath turning
the earth we walk to the clam spitting place
which pulls us like a tide.
teaching respect, tolerance, & humor.
circles drawn in sand by grass & wind.

putting light in those unlit eyes.
tumbles – stumbles – falls.   the comfort of an icy bed.
the weather is an open grave, the wind some last lost
breath. the strength & length of your body
arms folded like a scowl.

how it is that this brown paper bag is a ceremony?

sky curved & silent as a shoulder
the civil guard spurring the sky,
even the stars breaking into
morning. Nibbling at death with Bacchus
& his sweet numbness stretched from when
the sea was a child. no wisdom in any of the
glasses. madness like a blue white horse
curling along the sands. among the thistles
& the nettles, blackberry vines arching into
the brackish water at the mouth of the creek.
tomorrow's rocky love is a breeze through branches.
sleeping the lament of machines, sadness & machines.
the earthworm sees his/her shadow & faints
beneath the sleeping trees, the faded lilies.
tired of battling the roots all day — all night
in fear of moles — the early robin.

As they Always Have

"Woman is her own landscape . . . "
Octavio Paz

this swarm of blackberries, this reaching wall
   of vining life/light, the fog which comes before
      the indistinct, the unnamed/
      the brushstroke of geese against the sky.
breeze sucks at the shoreline & the willows.
what makes us think that it's true?
     & why must we try?

anamorphosis. each object throws
shadows which we call reality in its presence.
precipitating time—subliming gravity—or evanescing
at the feeling of life. urgent & immanent.
moment from moment torn, measured, secured,
a vision of pitiless reality, "rigor not brilliance.
/the machines are delirious."

empty suits illuminated by their own gas
desire turns as a physical force, tormenting the gears
tormented by years. each subject to perspective
the whorls of geometry, time, & gravity.
"emancipated metal" one tank of gasoline love.
a napalm-starred evening & kittens to boot.
lost in the shade of a corkscrew wandering
camp to camp inquiring of the Swiss Army.
a nostalgia for desire, the night hushed down.
& creases on your heels. diamonds in the souls
of her shoes. Chitlan streets.

the slow turning ritual of absence
glass delayed in its falling
a new innovation: The Jesus Bar.
modesty clothed in a touch of malice
unfolded & wound again in folds
disappearing with a pirouette.
the bees are dancing the direction of the falling
sun. faith that it is good.

"naked, lonely, & cold."
Sharon Doubiago

all of these drowned stories coming from her
hair. she says that not all roads grow wider.
sleep & death: the night furred between your thighs
seeing the journey—these steps—is the journey.
Dead Indian Road they call it still Dead Indian Road.

the light suffering into colors, the night into desire
she crushes midnight between her thighs.
"a danger is greatest when we fail each other."
her heart is a small town with a single monument.
she smiled me a cupful of moonlight.

the ache of needing to travel & traveling
in the need. This breath of stars
twining in her greying hair.
"Flowers bloom when they know they're dying."

In the skin of an epiphany
she calls my name & the world continues
turning. she turns those pale blue lamps
like glass shattering, a stutter of stars
crossing over. the breath shaping her body.
we are cutting down the clouds, milling them.

the wind, also, aches to remember the stars
those whirling stars. blessed by other stars.
faces like constellations also spinning in
darkness, nebula in the firmament
illness is a dark voice, a thirst in his head.
it is such a singing place—such a song of light
into a snarl & flickering darkness
a sky gone the color of love & breathing light
a night star-dense & clear. coyotes on the wind
each dream adds a star to the sky
an irresistible sky which softens the earth.
my heart is a tortured bird, caged & lonely
tearing against the hills of her body
pale blue & darkness. the way it was before us.
not anatomy, but culture which makes us human.
art, language, technology; religion
unfolding the human being within us.

the herons are leashed to their shadows
tied there to the whirling ground.

bells & chimes in the tops of fir trees.
hope & light eaten by the rage of sunset.
fruit flies gather at the rim of my wineglass.
the flames migrate from my heart downwards.
this must be love. though the weather dies each day.
death is a ticking crocodile hook. for herons
though the night is webbed, their feet are not.

she knows she is pregnant through the smell of
camellias and the thin grey rain.
she chambers a prayer to the pistol. if
napalm is a gospel, fire also is a prayer,
and the camellia's mute & filled with bright light.
she is pious & social in her laughter.
bringing down this house of ribs.

the wires whisper us together grey crowding
the new fall sky. silence rises as steamy
mist from the creekbed. the geese contemplate
their long migration south—the weight of
hummingbirds--& they remember the Sound's mild
past winters, "There is no use fishing."

false words, though the fish are torpid & fast.
the wind folds the fields & stores them for spring,
the leaves begin to lace the summer's comfort.
the frost is moving south & down the mountain
sides. & the spiders begin to move inside
it is their desperation to survive.

the rain takes off its clothes, glues ours
to our damp skins. each breath fogs
before us like a memory. & the golden carp
sink into their own landscape. time runs
out of each bottle, fills our lungs & empties our glass.
the night laces its gloves & delivers the velvet dawn.

domesticity is an avalanche of responsibility.
smoke bites the bullet—the bullet bites the belly.
it is what we need to know. awaiting the bone white
angels. the sea is downstream it waits for
us all as it forever has, several ounces
of salts our total value. the arpeggio of trees
& grace-notes fall though the ferns abide
though the night eats the trees among the hush
of blackberries—the thrash & burn of nettles.

I gather the small stones—sift the roots from the
soil—passion & foolishness—ruin & indifference.
weighing the anchor; hand over hand; to scale
thunder, the cicatrice of lightning—a bruise
& a scar. like speech is a fragment of thought.
& thought some lost spark of light.
history bloodies our mouths in the Balkans.
our hands dancing on the mirror & smoke
our children's hands on the joystick guiding
the not so smart bombs to the banquet.
death & fire like a videogame from
                    several thousand feet.

stone upon stone wounding the alphabet
& preaching peace. his women fill the
house with bloodied rags each change of
the moon. he burns them & puts the ashes
on his garden. is this war? the rivers
& his own creek don't seem to notice.
it is breathing here —there it is death.

the daughters of midnight bearing their unwanted
children—the gifts of ethnic conflict & cleansing.
each new threat turning into a constellation
lost among all those turning stars.
here also—one god is no damn comfort at all.
the stars a field of death—the light glinting
from new stones. the killdeer runs the beach
stitching water & land & air together.

fish understand the theory of a knife
for them it is real & gut-felt.

each leader sure he is the lion of the lounge
the innocents are gathered together & sigh.
it is claimed that these houses were not made for
humans (but by them) surely. if the moon
is an emery wheel our nights could be
smooth ground glass & the rain would
wash our morals clean, white, pure.

she spreads guilt in the night, built on
dreams & those seven unconscious sins
in which judgement is passed as a shadow
dappled grey & cold, gone like fish & stars
sealed by justice, etched blood burning
into the sidewalks, fishing for echoes, reasons.
a motive. the hooves of butterflies trample my
garden as the wine wrinkles time
& humiliation undresses laughter
in a today where even used kidneys are not unemployed
& lost children must hide on the quaking streets,
life after birth "placenta of cocaine"
each mirror is a circular journey
& the sea sends no regrets, returns on time,
twice each day. each good intention is
its own punishment. sin has lost seven
deadly maps, running red with roses,
their secrets. the stars drink from the
creek & the Sound is a mirror flat.
the heron sleeps on paper as she is etched there.
shot silk blues & divestiture, to nudity
like a mandolin, so tuned that roses also
drop their petals, once upon a time,
then, naked without rhyme.

having learned to lie, we will
not. the bottle climbed to bed
& he changed each channel.

good intentions twist our words &
love has a defense though we cannot
name it now. right now,
the deer in the fields are unshining
the hour, nibbling the windfall apples.

the stars are seeds in a garden of sky
couplets resting at the firehouse waiting
for the fire, sparks in a new fall afternoon.

the wine of the day browsing among nettles
spending the day like bus change mixing vinegar
& pearls. this sin is seven surrenders
reaching the distance of summer grass
the brooding condemnation
of the church's voting right
wings dark tipped by winter & the gingham
the calico of shame. Saturday in the backseat
Sunday in the choir.   we cross each street of
strangers. & these seven sins hold up the holy roof
midnight & a candle. seven impenitent sins.
we are not wooden & we will gladly sin again.

I borrow the money to bury my father
& I haven't left his coffin yet
some tenor & blankness at losing his touch
failing to save him for always.

though I bless you for the wake I struggle in,
I ache here in your blood & love the air.
crickets & frogs from my garden tell me it's
all ok. it all remains simple & happening.

my father & I still share a glass of wine
a dream or two though he never taught me
to weld. he assures me I exist.
something still absurd & serious about surviving
in history, a ring of rivers & rains to come.

things will turn up they always have.
clarity is its own punishment.
& breasts are sweet bags of tea.

having fallen through all of summer
the feathers flame an eagle into the fir.
the light rests inside a sleeping girl's blouse
a shudder & a smile under the lawn of sleep.

where only the dust lives forever
the wind blows the grey morning from the trees.
the hearth/the fire pit was orphaned by his death.

the moon is vapor thin among the shadows
of trees, softening each night.
water is running everywhere.
the fish wake & move up Judd Creek.
they are sure that all air is thin & dangerous.

the icicles have fallen & the sky is chanting rain
in the wake of smoking campfires
sad ways in a small world.

nates. natez. buttocks.

nowanights the moon is waning
   the days are growing long
& she made the sidewalks shiver with desire.

each death assures continuity as each birth.
virus as the last defense the wild earth has
against man, dormant & innocuous, benign until
their appointed time, required, slow & late.

such a rain will take your breath away.
these hours of life are more awesome than death.
having no future one day death will manage
to call — life teaches living.
we owe life nothing; now or ever
it will still drag us away: anything
   but happiness.

the thing that really chips my nail polish
is that Ben Franklin who discovered electricity
found a toad which had been
hibernating several million years
   and revived it. so, it is possible to find
a living dinosaur. with this frayed logic
do you understand the immense quantity of
money/funding that it takes to remain poor?
all the light will turn the world when
   speech is extinguished. So, now
the bed is burning; the lights are going out.

"abandon all hope when you enter me." she proclaims

trying always to get free of what we've done.
the sun is a nest of doubts which burns
the eyes in the dark. sleeping if the sun will go
killing each topic intentionally, though nothing
keeps the stars off. & we've been flesh from the beginning.
we'll chase a drunk up every tree & down again;
one party pardoned for each fallen from a tree.
blessed by a frail hint of love before a timely death.
this knowledge forces us to make up love,
an act against oblivion.

he very nearly dreams his life, or this is what
he dreams, a belly full of stained glass
& god, the fear of evolution changes us.
rich ladies & their little dogs — quivering —
alone with uncertain stars & a steady meal.
fighting the wind to own a kite, cornering the sky
& laughing after the dance with other women.
I'm a stranger now, and you're gonna change too.

baldness like a gold tooth in a smile
spent this summer dusting the nettles.
cities bursting out of their budgets
sipping the brandy of the damned. saucily.

neap tide & a sea-raged landscape.

each wound leaves a scar, though some heal well.
each step is a step to the stars, & tideless.
searching the tinted color of afternoon
in shadows as long as a man's work day
as urban renewal strangles the poor folk downtown.
a photo that makes my hands bleed
unhappiness turns around and is as real
as missing the bus or the century
winding down. beside the garden
& the butterfly's bushes.

the stars are repairing the night among nettles
resting on the inner harbor, the dark narrow
grey path besides the creek. its final wild purity.
wallowing in the wet look of the northwest
when someone's left you, you can't help but be
there. the stars huddle together on the harbor
everywhere the guns raise wet promises & red.
while the city stirs & the moon rises
& the drive-by rides fill with the newly dead
whose love has warped their hearts under
streetlights & falling brick.

the seasons soften our lives, one wet, one dry,
the morning weaves itself through our clothing
clings to our coffee cups. & steams
    these torments of the heart.
obsidian flakes of fury
    swimming through these words like traffic.

time fate, and strange ways
through this blood bruised history of city.
haunted by the Pleiades & Venus,
a sleek coolnessed self possessed by beauty
the dreams run blood & wake obsessed
by that gravid curve of sky cold
chalked by dark-winged military planes
and payloads lumbering home. to land stolen
from the native wildlife & people.

as the night grows cool it touches them little
& the stars not at all. innocence gone long by
the boards & guilt unestablished.
hauling scant supplies into the darkness
where the outcast shadows of cats seek their
own solace, the hungry despair of the abandoned,
the streets of night are severe & hungry
among the brambles & the vacant lots.
but they will try to get you to dream.

the police themselves plotting judicious murder
in the name of traffic control & community
betterment, lust for change & progress.
god's sanity walks the streets begging spare
change, avoiding death one drink at a time.
dreaming seas of wine & blondes, then only wine
& seizures, purely resisting gravity, refusing
to exist in time — late for their own death
not knowing when to stop, surrender.
like dew melts away each mourning
polishing the motorcycle cop's boots bright.
pumping bullets into sighs,
it rains in paradise tonight
though I spend late summer drying apples & plums.

"a man, a woman, & a relationship.
But the cat . . . "
                              Peter Porter

ransacking the genius of the universe
stretched at the edge of reluctant poverty
the wasps mad all through the dangerous summer
her discontent was a fearlessly truthful art.

it shielded her from despair though she fed the days
her tears & her tears she fed the days.
doubt overcasting each sky under which she lived.
forgiveness in the garden—there we go to forgive

ourselves. tend the innocence of plants.
tossing anger to the compost, nettles to the tea.
her hand opens the envelope—mine shakes.
waiting at the hospice, one hand searching

the other, for death, nightingale among dirty linens
panties & bras, the sisters of the quail tilt
their hats & adjust. though people cry &
moan; the cat is dancing literally.

" . . . what the gods mean by words
goes the long way round or takes on flesh
in dreams."   Peter Porter

clothed in syntax, naked to the core suffering
nocturnal commissions, shadows & the sublime
hunger shifts its claws. morphine & hot
chocolate. like love is the cadence of memory.
wooly bears humping through the garden.
taking an ax to the memory
she coughs up this little stone of unhappiness.
I carry it in my pocket, shine it with my sweat.
I lean its way. pardoned by a lack of power.
shifting cautiously on this killing ground.
at least I'm perfect in my genes
seeking some week with a Tuesday, still.
& wading through the dales of death.

eloquence & decency unawakenable, depressed dies
early.   better to be awake than be forced to dream.
loving ourselves towards death & loving it so.
our feelings glow among us, death in small print
she goes to the legend; he sits in the kitchen, empty.
the cats do not despise us; they are not disappointed.
it is no small thing to die. shitty luck.
twisting the ingredients of sorrow
searching for the mystery which chokes us.
with this I swallow my penance. life
is an improvement upon death. "a tit-bit close
to me," it is the mystery which
daunts us. she wears her suffering
& punishment is the same as law.
ego is a ministry: tell them about bad luck.
laying long & warmly. rhyming in color.

like scraps of sound balanced in the wind
the fish leaping to swallow the moon.
carving the wooden memory
trying to remember where I've planted the trilliums.

most kids are desperate to play
          crossing the rubble of dreams
aching for an apology while the time
ticks by on our wrists. watch or pulse.
the rent is paid; the streets quiet enough
& the dreams still rise to the sky, cloudy.

nursing dereliction & buying the right clothes.
enduring the burden of our songs.
always we are somewhere, though anywhere
is what drags our blood. the ground is
worth more than we are. rot & promise
that's the clambeds & the smell of life,
changing, herons from the glass of evening
with their purposeful flight.
all of us lose arguments with the river.
all of us cast these long thin lines.
Dead men in the office gambling with other lives.
thoughts race the moon for darkness, & darkness
wins.

reinventing & transforming

fishing on the shores of grief, a dark bed
of river and hours and thirst burning.
the crisp sound of autumn whirling in the wind.
some cemeteries are not lonely
for those of us trying to stay in our skins
as damp as the misted leaves.
whining & whirling like a wounded wheel.
hardly able to burn the days for heat enough.
wood smoke and tidewater's sweet smell. scent
this science of stars & shivering shadows
saved up for the darkest nights.
so tired of chastity feeding our blood
to the days. the beaches eaten by heavy rain
& the tides, dying between knives & the night.
Macchu Picchu burning. the hungry besieged
by food & swat teams, lack of sleep, a dark
black cup cradled in their shaking hands.
blood in the cradle. rock-a-bye. the soil itself
acts up—remembers some other rules, resting
near wine. wrapped for burial in the dawn wind.
Fragrant language!? " . . . a snout full of ooze & silence."
blend guitars & lost feathers. something there is
in the eye of a wheel — less motion,
a contentment there in its turning.
drowning the mountains in falling stars.
the butterflies tremble where there are no emeralds.

transparencies

the kingfisher's feathers tremble with anticipation
as the tide turns once again. grapes are
nature's way of moving wine from the earth
into bottles. like a fish trapped by the wind
saturating the afternoon with sweat & foggy rain
the streets grow strange & more vague.
sinking into the evening & the rain wet soil, earth
ground. the streets are a naked well of pain.
the airiness of winter willows in a misted rain.

Is there no suffering too private?
each day is a mountain to be carried into
the sunset & each night a sea to wash
toward the dawn. maintaining a skeptical
mysticism. in the homesick ghetto,
searching for an echo chamber & a recording
contract. some poets, some writers, are afraid
of their own voices. dying so little in the afternoon.

washed away singing in the unceasing rain.
its incredible roof washing loving sounds.
if life were different suffering would be the same.
this morning costs nights, & this afternoon will cost days.
cold fear with breasts cuddles next to me in sleep.
a man can kill perfectly, & he will die.
carried through life to heaven by our own bad luck.
retrieving the startled morning.
blood pools like guilt on the sidewalk. spills
to the street. blaming this gypsy heart for its pain.
judging the height of the stars by the tallest trees
while the anger of the poor grows like lost seeds,
doubt & confidence, the eighth deadly sins.
the corpses of the poor keep on dying each breath.

Get It?

the enflamed heart strikes anywhere, matches fire to
the rippled line of horizon. stillness becomes pervasive
& the light shrinks from darkness. & the crows are
still telling that same old joke, quite pleased to share
it and cackle/laugh in their dark wings of light.
wings of flight. while the chickadees listen, cock their
heads (glittered eyes) & listen. binding together the
separate links—this same sad joke for tens of thousands
of year—generations & generations of crows—something
about flying. to their fledglings. to the coyotes.
to the stellar jays. the same one fine joke. they
demure. falling like feathered stones from their purchase
a sheen of coins, a skein of eggs for the salmon
black angels with their long-kept secret, oblique flight.
carrying this one joke, hackneyed, through centuries
remaking the telling each new year in their bright eyes.
arriving new each new day with the same joke & the dawn
something about the old forests, the old growth & ancient
eyes celebrating the need to tell this one important thing
passing on the humor & steering among the stars.
this final clarity of summer pausing towards the equinox.
got to tell it one more time & eyes like beaded stone.
"say, did you hear the one about . . . "

"lifting the spine"
"finding the spine"
"breaking the spine"

sparkled warm without fire. the text dreams itself perfect
bound in cloth & glue. "In the beginning was the book store."
& the book store was void and without form
neither was it alphabetized nor ordered by subject matter.

push the muse lady back into traffic; the light has changed.
the vortex of her eyes, the vertigo of her breath, the verisimilitude
of her charmed body—her charms through the rearview mirror.
she leaves me alone & in fever – in order to break.
she raises a calypso kitten. I beat my wings, rub my legs
together, dance. & she still does not see. So I attempt
to usurp the dawn. one more failure among many. no music.

sometimes everything is in your head; though it is just as real.
out there in the distance, somewhere, is forever & ever.
& nothing is too much fun. tongues filled with the taste of
dance. give up the language, just smell to me.
I finished it tomorrow. I will do it yesterday. I will
have finished it by three. death does not stop. here.
liquid dances. love, earth, and darkness.
eyes like rainwater falling.

Carving the gods into wood, this way they will burn.
it's where all the old gods have gone. my life is alive
with blood. it was a dark & rain lashed night.
is an owl in your dreams the same as an owl?

her mind was like another layer of skin & he was
shedding her. all of the critters take the narrow path.
something here in this room has fallen out of a dream.
though he had a shadow longer than tomorrow, it was today.
& his body moves with her heart. a smile like a frozen plain.
As the day went on—the night goes down to breasts
& navel, every stitch, fastened like darkness to her crevices.
Half-hidden wounds healing like a hoarse whisper towards
the morning. There is a wondering creature inside her.
Nothing that the tears wash away really would have stayed.
she has died & my nails are still growing & the earth scratches
my fingers. The night, like darkness, flies through the child
& no echoes come. how is it that birth cries & sings?

Tracking Indian Creek

a bloodless man in a bloodied field. still, cold, from the
hunt. Finding Indian Creek: sure it had been there
year after regular year before. strewn with coyote scat
and bear paws fishing with the wind. The golden eagle
trailing the heron. his blues or his fish the object.
& of all the concern. the flooded creek packed & moved in
near the cliffs & deep water of their shadows. each
of us growing quietly desperate. startled dismay may
strain awareness. a heart beating still within this pallid
bleeding thing. death & deathless peace at each end of the
string. stars like a carpet of prayers. stars like
this one time beach of sand.

no human hand might have touched this misted rock &
water fall. umbrellaed by the rock-strewn trees. Canyon
wind like an oven through the mist. The creek gone cinematic.
& water fall dramatic. serenity crosses the river to escape.
May that buds and blossoms is gone, the summer leaving too.
September when the sweet plums fall will even soon be through.
& the trees will be bare as a coed's legs. though there's
nothing better this side of the grave & no one leaves alive
life is a web of shining days & butterflies catching the
slight updraft were not a dream.

www.ingramcontent.com/pod-product-compliance
Lightning Source LLC
Chambersburg PA
CBHW062213080426
42734CB00010B/1869